10 90

3 ✓ S0-BRQ-172

AUTHOR'S PREFACE.

———

This is intended to be a brief or compendium of a larger volume on Mr. Garland which is to follow at some later date, when the author may have the time and money to hunt out other records, and write up still other phases of the great Arkansan's noble life.

TABLE OF CONTENTS

A Life of Mr. Garland

OF ARKANSAS

A Thesis for the Master's Degree

By FARRAR NEWBERRY, A. M.

𝔇𝔢𝔡𝔦𝔠𝔞𝔱𝔢𝔡

TO THE CITIZENS OF THE STATE
1908

B G

A.H. Garland,
Little Rock,
Ark.s "

AUGUSTUS HILL GARLAND.

SECTION I

It is not the province of the biographer to indulge in exorbitant praise—still less that of the thesis-writer to employ excessive flattery. The writer is not unaware that the written history of a man, whose life exhibits no adventures, save of an intellectual kind, is seldom read with that enthusiasm which is generally called forth by the story of a chieftain. Readers at large are more fond of tracing the progress of action than of thought, although the latter is the source of the former. They can gaze with rapture upon the beauty or magnificence of the stream, without caring to understand the mysteries of the power by which the fountain spray is thrown up from its secret home. The achievements of the great intelligencies of the age are too little regarded. If mankind would but mark the gradual unfolding of the principles, powers, and passions of the great master spirits, as indeed they are coming more and more to do in our day than ever before, each generation could be furnished with an amount of moral power by which it might elevate itself into a nobler sphere of being, and leave behind it a long train of glory for the illumination of posterity.

The most fitting monument in honor of a public man is a faithful record of his public acts. If these acts be worthy, and the record simple, time, which destroys all things but good deeds and lofty thoughts, will embalm them for eternity. If they be base, "eulogy adds a lie to their deformities," and they must perish of their own disease. In the spirit of this truth we address ourselves to the task before us, seeking but to write a plain and simple record of a plain and simple life.

Augustus Hill Garland was born in Tipton County, Tenn., June 11, 1832. Both his parents were from good families, and dated their ancestry back to Revolutionary times. His mother's people, the Hills, were from Franklin County, near Louisburg, and his father had been christened Rufus by his Revolutionary sire, in Virginia, who was from a highly respectable family.

An incident happened a few months after the birth of Augustus H. Garland that probably determined the parents to come to Arkansas, and hence to give to that State the great man about whom this book is written. This incident, otherwise trivial, will bear noting here. Rufus and his good wife had a fine farm in Tipton County, and were doing well. However, he had his fault—a grievous one—but one that hurt himself more than anyone else. He, in common with other Tennesseans, went to the County Seat every monthly county court, and, after all business was over, indulged himself too freely with the juice of the corn. Rufe Garland sober was the pink of courtesy and manhood; but drunk, he, like most others, was anything but that. The home-keepers of Tipton soon came to know his ways, and in the late afternoon of all county court days every door went shut and stayed closed until he was out of town.

He was cured in a peculiar way. One Saturday evening, he started home, and at about the half-way point, he passed a place where a body of campers had built their night fire. Riding violently through the camp, he became engaged in a broil with a young man, and, in an infuriated state, stabbed him. When Garland saw him fall, he was sobered—he was Rufe Garland, the gentleman. He did all he could for him, and was much grieved over the affair. He was arrested, however, and put in the Tipton jail, and the injured young man lingered between life and death. It was a terrible punishment for him. He employed his time in making all kinds of tin instruments; and chiefest of them, he constructed a tin fiddle, and with it he entertained the citizens of Tipton with his music, which, it is said, was really entrancing. The young man whom Rufe had cut got well, and became a listener to his fiddling. It so impressed him that he forgave him, slipped out into the great world and rejoined his people in Missouri, saying that he would never prosecute a man who could make music like that.

Garland was released, but he came out of jail a changed man. He then, feeling the necessity of moving away from this scene, sent his wife and young son, Augustus, then a year old, together with Elizabeth, John, and Rufus King, the other children, to Arkansas, with the assurance that he was done with whiskey—a resolution which he actually lived out during the remaining few years of his life. When he had sold all the possessions, he followed to Arkansas, and is said to have made one of the best citizens of his section. They came to a place on Red river, near what is now Garland City. In a short while the father died, and the family moved to Spring Hill, in Hempstead County. Upon the boyhood of Gus Garland, we shall not dwell at length. His father died a few years after they came, and his mother, strong both mentally and morally, gave her son an elementary education at home. They continued to live at Spring Hill until Augustus was twelve years of age, when they moved to Washington, Ark. As a small boy he was prepared

for college partly in the private academy of H. R.
Banks, and perhaps under another school-master,
named Day. At fourteen he was sent by his mother
to Bardstown, Ky., then the most famous seat of learn-
ing in the Southwest, where he pursued his academic
studies in the Catholic Schools of St. Mary and St.
Joseph. He took a thorough course of training, receiv-
ing the degree, and also doing some post-graduate
work. While there, he read law a great deal, as was
the custom in those days, for ambitious young men.
He attended courses in the court room when he could.
At that time the local bar was very strong, and Garland profited greatly by this practice.

Returning home, he went to Sevier County at nine-
teen, to teach school for a year, in order to prepare
himself better for the law, and get general experience.
It is said that while teaching at this early age, he was
brought before a circuit court by one of the patrons of
his school, for whipping the latter's child; but he
plead his own case, and was acquitted.

In 1853 he was admitted to practice law at Washington, Ark., just after he married Miss Virginia
Sanders, which event took place when he was twenty-
one, just upon his advent to manhood. Virginia Sanders was a brilliant young woman of an old family of
Virginia, and herself beautiful, cultured, and tactful,
She was the daughter of Simon T. Sanders, who for
thirty years was Clerk of Hempstead County. Garland
read law with several lawyers at Washington, while
acting as Deputy Clerk under his father-in-law. He
thus learned much that was useful in his after life,
and more than all else, the great lesson of patient
labor, which few men learn too well, and which, in
fact, lays the foundation for all permanent greatness
and worth. Nearly all of his time was devoted to the
prosecution of legal studies, and to the general disci-

plining of his mind, which training he still felt to be very incomplete. His mother had in the meantime married Major Hubbard, afterward Circuit Judge, and a very prominent lawyer at Washington; and Garland thus had the legal opportunities afforded by his father-in-law's office. They organized the firm of Hubbard and Garland, which continued for a few years, and was one of the strongest in South Arkansas. Young Garland is said to have been always found sitting up with a law book at night, and of course throughout the day. Some one asked him one day, "would he never put down that book?" "Not until I have reached the office of Attorney General of the United States," was the reply. Later pages will tell how he actually did occupy that place.

By 1856 Mr. Garland had advanced considerably in his knowledge of the law. His mental talents were even then beginning to come out. He had laid well his foundation; he had made careful preparation; and, moving to Little Rock, he formed a law partnership with a Mr. Ebenezer Cummins. Mr. Cummins, besides being a law partner with Garland, was also in the firm of Pike and Cummins, also in Little Rock. One day in March, 1858, Cummins was found dead in his bed, from some sudden cause. Mr. Garland was left practically alone to manage the ever-increasing business of both these firms, and the responsibility thus thrust upon him was great. He was then quite a young man, beardless and unskilled, but ever alert and diligent, The business took him into counties where he had never been before. The way he sustained himself, so that his clients almost without exception, found it unnecessary to employ assistance for him, is nothing less than wonderful. A young man of strong mind and great energy, he advanced rapidly in his profession. His habits were notably studious and systematic.

He was analytical and searching, and possessed untiring energy, clear perception, and inexorable logic. His preparation of his cases was always exhaustive. He soon became thoroughly versed in the literature of his profesion. He had resource, grasp, and above all, the sense of justice. Even at this early time, Mr. Garland was able to carry with him into the arena of the court room much of that judicial temperament that enables one to perceive both sides of questions brooking discussion—a faculty which long and assiduous practice at the bar tends most strongly to cultivate, and one that added greatly to his success in the fields of endeavor, and gave a certain unity to his career, varied as it was and full of vicissitudes. This faculty enabled him to preserve the same equanimity in victory or defeat.

One thing that contributed very largely to Mr. Garland's early success in his profession of the law, was that he was capable of doing an immense amount of work without apparent hurry or fatigue. Though quick to sieze and analyze the most complex details of fact, and to apply appropriate legal principles; and though his memory of both was remarkably retentive and his legal knowledge very extensive, yet he never trusted to the inspiration of the moment, but placed his main reliance upon uncompromising labor.

In the court room, as elsewhere, he was of a very kindly and tolerable disposition. He took men as he found them, and never demanded ideal perfection in anyone. He was especially considerate through force of long habit, towards all who were connected with the administration of justice—officers, witnesses, and jurors. Always courteous towards his adversaries, he was likewise respectful and deferential toward the courts; and although it was said that he possessed the rare faculty of getting all that he desired out of a witness, yet he rarely gave offense even to those who were unduly sensitive. His fine sense of humor often relieved the tedium of legal proceedings, but never degenerated into buffoonery, and was never used to wound the feelings of others. Strong and forcible in his presentation of facts, eager and intent upon victory, his advocacy was a model of fairness; and if he could not win on the merits of his case, he never resorted to any questionable methods. In the court room or out of it, his manners were affable, simple, and unaffected. Mr. Garland, though still a young man, soon came to be recognized as one of the leading lawyers of the State. More of his characteristics and character is reserved until the end.

Through habits of close study Mr. Garland acquired an extraordinary familiarity with the decisions of the Supreme Court of the United States, and afterwards made use of them with striking effects. His acquaintance with them was not only thorough, but critical; hence it was entirely consistent with his habits of thought that he should prefer to practice at that high tribunal. As the years elapsed, Mr. Garland, after the great dispute over the "Iron-Clad Oath" law had been settled in his favor, came to have a profound respect for the Supreme Court, amounting almost to reverence. He was an enthusiastic admirer of Chief Justice Marshall, and had a great personal familiarity with the long line of decisions of the Supreme Court. Garland was first admitted to practice at that court on December 26, 1860.

In politics Mr. Garland was an old-line Whig, but afterwards when party names changed, and the Whigs were absorbed in the other parties, he represented his State as a Democrat. In 1861 he was elected to represent Pulaski County in the State Convention which voted for secession, and known as the Secession Convention of Arkansas. Though only twenty-nine years of age, he took a leading part among the conservatives in opposing radical action at the first session. Though an ardent Southerner, he nevertheless opposed secession, and exercised as much or more influence than any other member of that body; still he seldom spoke or made a motion. In fact, the Union men were on the defensive, and simply attempted to keep wrong from being done. A man of great sprightliness and versatility, he did not attempt oratory, according to Judge Corrigan, who is one of the four survivors of that Convention, writing from memory for the American Historical Review, Book I; but he used a colloquial and argumentative style that was attractive and convincing. He did not believe that the States should secede, and thought that the great calamity which was about to sweep his country to ruin and desolation was greatly maximized by unwonted and unnecessary agitation, and could yet be averted. Mr. Garland was, we believe, a Nationalist at heart, as opposed to being a Seceder. He believed that the South was right in holding that at the time of the framing of the Constitution sovereignty was believed by all to be divided; that the States, the original possessors of sovereignty, gave part of this, by donating certain sovereign powers, to the new-created nation. Sovereignty was then believed to be divisible; but decisions of the Supreme Court, from that time, began to mould the new idea of nationality into practical form. Mr. Garland's profound admiration for the decisions of the Supreme Court undoubtedly must have influenced him greatly. He, like Alexander Stephens, and others, did not agree with Mr. Davis, that the South had the absolute right to secede whenever it pleased. He threw the whole weight of the counsels and his great personality into the work of averting serious measures; but it was of no avail. The people were in too great a state of commotion, and too much action towards moderation on the part of the convention would likely have proved dangerous. As the realization dawned upon Mr. Garland that war was then inevitable, he was confronted with the problem of whether he should put his services to the task of further maintaining the Union and join the Union side in the coming conflict, or should take sides with his State and section. This grave question stared many great men of that time directly in the face. Hnudreds of men of prominence in public life had to choose between State and Union. It was with reluctance that Mr. Garland chose to cleave to the former and let go the latter. He voted against secession until the effort to re-enforce Fort Sumpter by the Federal Government, which brought on the attack upon that fort by the forces of the South. Then he reluctantly yielded and voted for secession, and from then on was a zealous supporter of the Confederate cause.

Mr. Garland was sent by his State as a delegate to the Convention known as the Provisional Convention, at Montgomery, Ala., in May, 1861. He was elected by the Secession Convention to represent Arkansas at Montgomery by fifty-two votes, the largest received by any of the five, (Garland, Johnson, Thomasson, Watkins and Rust.) He took a leading part in the arguments incident to the framing of the provisional Constitution of the Confederate States.

When he had finished service in that capacity he returned to Arkansas, and did some actual service in the trenches. This, however, did not last long; for his State had already become awake to his great ability, energy and patriotism; and he was called from service in the Army to hold a seat in the lower House of the Confederate Congress. He was chosen without opposition. When the Confederate Capital was moved from Montgomery to Richmond, Va., Garland carried his family with him to that place. In 1862 he was returned to the Congress, then at Richmond, and was re-elected again in 1864, but soon resigned to accept a seat in the Confederate Senate, made vacant by the death of Hon. Charles B. Mitchell.

As a member of the Confederate Congress Mr. Garland made his first really great reputation as a lawyer. In committee work, in debate, and in conference, he became one of the most influential men of that distinguished body. His war record was not made on the battlefield, but in a place where heroism was just as much needed. It is true that the South's heroes of the sixties were for the most part heroes of the physical battlefield. The noblest sons enlisted for the field, and comparatively few of manhood and merit remained to hold the helm of the ship of State. But Mr. Garland realized that fearless, honest men were needed in political offices then more than any other time; and so his services were in the civil halls of his country, and not upon the field. He could not have done a wiser thing; and more is the honor due him for it. The conflict for justice and freedom from selfish tendency was as great and terrible as any ever settled on a hard-fought battlefield. These men who held the places of civil trust in the South were, more than all the generals of the war, the index-fingers of the country's welfare. For Mr. Garland, therefore, it was an all-important matter that he guard the more carefully his every act and word, that it might redound to the glory of his State, and the good of the Confederacy's cause. The South's great Epic of the future, that will tell of the private Confederate soldier's last farewell to home, as he left to join the faded ranks of the gray; of the picket's last watch on earth, from which he entered into the death-watch. to guard his fallen comrades; of the fortitude, the self-sacrifice and matchless devotion of the daughters and wives, whose weapons were sacred prayer and sacred tears; of the faithful old slave, who carried the body of his dead master, wrapped in the flag he followed, and laid upon his own shield, to the sad ones at home—this "Iliad" of the future will also tell, with the imperishable history of a Livy, of the faithfulness and service of the devoted civilians of the Confederacy, who kept unstained throughout the struggle the escutcheon of her public dignity in a Congress which, though unrecognized by the National legislature, was yet her source of law and progress. Mr. Garland on one occasion many years later said that he had been prominently spoken of more than once for the place of Attorney General in the Confederate Cabinet.

At the close of the war Mr. Garland resumed the practice of law in Little Rock. On January 24, 1865, Congress passed a law prohibiting those who had aided the South from practicing in the United States Courts, without taking the "Iron-Clad Oath." This was a heavy blow to the leading lawyers of the South, and deprived them of one of their chief means of support. All Southerners felt that the law was unjust. Mr. Garland believed that Congress had no constitutional right to pass such a law, and resolved to test its validity in the United States Supreme Courts. He argued that it was invalid, producing one of the most powerful, forceful and clearest briefs of argument ever made before that high tribunal. He won his case, and the law was set aside by the court on account of its unconstitutionality. This was a great victory for Mr. Garland, and won for him a national reputation as a lawyer. This successful effort to secure readmission to the United States Courts without the iron-clad test oath, was one of the most notable contests ever waged there. The victory gave Mr. Garland high prestige in his State, as well as a national reputation, and resulted in his election to the ·United States Senate in 1867, though he was not permitted to take his seat. Owing to the importance of the case, we submit a report of notes on the proceedings of the same, as given in 4 Wallace of the United States Supreme Court Reports.

Mr. Garland had been permitted to practice before the Supreme Court of the United States in 1860. His name remained on the roll of the Supreme Court Attorneys from then until 1865, but the Rebellion intervened, and all the business in which he was concerned at the time of his admission remained indisposed of. Having taken part in the Rebellion by being in the Congress of the "so-called" Confederate States, from May, 1861, until the surrender, first in the lower House and afterwards in the Senate, he could not take the oath prescribed by Congress, before mentioned, and the rule of the court itself, of March, 1865. Arkansas, in May, 1861, seceded and attached herself to the Confederacy. In July, 1865, Garland received from President Johnson a pardon, which granted "full pardon and anmesty for all ogenses committed in the Rebellion, and conditioned as follows: The pardon to take effect from the day on which the said A. H. Garland shall take the oath prescribed in the proclamation of the President, dated May 29, 1865; and to be void and of no effect if the said A. H. Garland shall hereafter at any time acquire any property whatever in slaves, or make use of slave-labor." Mr. Garland took the oath and faithfully pledged himself to support the constitution, and all laws made during the Rebellion with reference to the emancipation of slaves.

Garland produced his pardon, and by petition filed in court, asked permission to continue to practice as an attorney and counsellor of the court, without taking the oath required by the Act of January, 24, 1865, and the rule of the court. He rested his application principally on the grounds: (1) That the act of January 24, 1865, so far as it affected his status in the court, was unconstitutional and void; and (2) that if the act were constitutional, he was released from compliance with its provisions by the pardon of the President. Messrs. Reverdy Johnson and M. S. Carpenter argued for the petitioner, Mr. Garland, who had filed a brief of his own, presenting fully his case:

I. The act of January 24, 1865, was an ex post facto law. Suppose "A" tomorrow commits assault and battery. Tomorrow, say, Congress passes a law that no person shall hold any office of honor or profit until he shall have taken an oath that he has never committed that crime. Is it not apparent that such an act, in its practical operation, would be ex post facto, as adding to the punishment of assault and battery an important penalty not attaching when the crime was committed? This is only an illustration of the proposition that an act is unconstitutional, which accomplishes a result forbidden by the Constitution.

II. That is the result accomplished by the act complained of, and how does that result accord with the spirit and provisions of the Constitution? The act of Congress of January 24, 1865, accomplishes a result in direct opposition to the constitutional effect of the pardon. The President says, "You shall not be excluded from practicing in the Supreme Court in consequence of your crime; I pardon you." The act of Congress says, "You shall never practice in the Supreme Court without taking an oath which will be perjury, and then, on conviction of that, that shall disqualify you." The Constitution provides that the President "Shall have power to grant reprieves and pardons for all offenses against the United States, except in cases of impeachment." The effect of the pardon is to make the offender a new man. Therefore the effect of the pardon is to make it impossible for any power on earth to inflict, constitutionally, any punishment whatsoever upon the petitioner for the crime of treason specified in the pardon.

III. The act, as applied to the petitioner, visits upon him a punishment of his pardoned crime.

(1) The pardon absolves him from all punishment for his offense.

(2) The act in question does, in its operation on him, disfranchise him from holding office.

(3) Such disfranchisement is a punishment for which he has been pardoned.

(4) Therefore, the act and the pardon are in conflict, and the pardon must prevail.

IV. What right has Congress to prescribe other qualifications than are found in the Constitution? Congress can exercise none but delegated powers. If this act be constitutional, there is no limit to the others which may be hereafter prescribed.

The petitioner's rights to practice in the Federal Courts is property. He has a vested right in his office as an attorney, of which he can only be deprived by some regular judicial proceeding. Depriving the petitioner, therefore, of his office, by an enforcement of this act of Congress, is depriving him of his property without due process of law.

Mr. R. H. Marr, of Louisiana, had filed a similar petition, and he also presented an argument for Mr. Garland. Mr. Speed, Attorney General of the United States, argued for the constitutionality of the act:

"The privilege of practicing law is not a natural right, but a privilege created by the law, and according to its conditions. If Congress could present the old oath of 1789 to Attorneys, why can it not prescribe the present one? Cannot the legislature prescribe the qualifications which the counsellor shall have? Where is the limit?

"As to the expediency and propriety of such an act as that of January 24, 1865, that involves a question of duty in Congress, with which this court has nothing to do. It would seem that, in times such as we have had, some oath ought to be required that would keep from this bench and bar men who had been guilty, and more than guilty, of treason."

Mr. Stanbery, special counsel for the United States, also argued against admitting Mr. Garland. His point was, that pardon is forgiveness, but not necessarily restoration, and that Congress had the right to pass the act, and the Court to pass its rule. Then he discussed the expediency of Congress' passing the said law. He stated that the law was eminently and positively expedient at the time.

The brilliant argument of Mr. Reverdy Johnson, in reply to the argument of the opposition ends with a thrilling and somewhat eloquent conclusion. We give both argument and conclusion, briefly:

I. The law in question, in its application to Mr. Garland, is an ex post facto law. However criminal his conduct may have been, and however liable he may have been to prosecution, the particular punishment inflicted by the act of 1865, could not have been amended. He could not have been convicted for not taking that oath, or any other, but only "upon the testimony of two witnesses, to the same overt act, or on confession in open court."

II. The act is also in conflict with that part of the constitution (the fifth article of the amendments), which provides that "no person shall be compelled, in any criminal case, to be a witness against himself, nor be deprived of life, liberty and property, without due process of law."

III. The act is void because it interferes with the rights and powers conferred on the Judiciary Department of the government, by the third Article of the Constitution. The admission of counsel is a prerogative of the court, and cannot be interferred with by any other department of the government.

IV. The answer to the argument of the opposition that the privilege of practicing before a court is not a "natural right" is, that the very preservation of liberty itself demands the aid of counsel. The safety of the citizen depends on the lawyer. The Courts also require their aid. Congress would, therefore, but convert themselves into a semblage of tyrants, regardless of the safety of the citizens, recreant to the cause of freedom, and forgetful of the guarantees of the constitution, if they attempted to deny to the courts and to the citizens the assistance of counsel.

V. Even conceding the constitutionality of the act, Mr. Garland is removed from its operation by the President's pardon, with the terms of which he has complied.

In conclusion, Mr. Johnson said:

"May it please the court, every right-minded man— I should think every man who has within his bosom a heart capable of sympathy—who is not the slave to a narrow political feeling—a feeling that does not embrace as it ought to do, a nation's happiness; must make it the subject of his daily thoughts and of his prayers to God, that the hour may come, and come soon, when all the States shall be again within the protecting shelter of the Constitution and Union— enjoying, all of them, its benefits; contented, happy, and prosperous; sharing, all of them, in its duties; devoted, all, to its principles, and participating alike in its renown; that the hour when former differences shall be forgotten, and nothing remembered but our ancient concord and the equal title we have to share in the glories of the past, and to labor together for the still greater glories of the future, may soon come. And, may I not, with truth, assure your honor, that this result will be hastened by the bringing within these courts of the United States a class of men, now excluded who, by education, character and profession, are especially qualified by their example to influence the public sentiment of their respective States, and to bring those states to the complete conviction, which it is believed they most largely entertain, that to support and defend the Constitution of the United States, and the government instituted by it, in all its rightful authority, is not only essential to their peoples' happiness, but is a duty to their country and their God."

The arguments concluded, Mr. Justice Field delivered the judgment of the court:

"The exaction of the oath that the party has never taken part in nor aided any movement against, the United States, is the mode provided for ascertaining the parties on whom the act is intended to operate:

"The power of pardon conferred by the constitution on the President is unlimited except in cases of impeachment. It extends to every offence known to law, and may be exercised at any time after its commission, either before legal proceedings are taken, or during their pendency, or after conviction and judgment.

"A pardon reaches the punishment of the offense, and the guilt of the offender.

"The petitioner in this case (Mr. Garland), having received a full pardon for all offenses committed by his participation, direct or otherwise, in the Rebellion, is relieved from all penalties and disabilities attached to the offense of treason, committed by such participation. For that offense he is beyond the reach of punishment of any kind. He cannot, therefore, be excluded by reason of that offense, from continuing the enjoyment of a previously acquired right to appear as an attorney and counsellor in the Federal Courts.

Mr. Justice Miller, in behalf of himself and the Chief Justice, Mr. Chase, and Messrs. Justices Swayne and Davis, delivered a dissenting opinion.

In a little book written in 1898, and entitled "Experiences in the Supreme Court," Mr. Garland humorously relates of the getting of his pardon, and of the great case, as follows: "In July, 1865, I called on President Johnson with much amiability, and requested pardon for my deeds of omission and commission in the row; and, seconded by the efforts of my constant and steadfast friend, Mr. Reverdy Johnson, I procured the pardon. It was large and capacious, and I hugged it closely and went off rejoicing with exceeding great joy, as a novus homo would naturally do. Before going home, however, I went to the Clerk's office and renewed a very pleasant acquaintance with those there, and formed others quite agreeable. I drew a petition and forwarded to President Johnson, and he filed it in the Supreme Court. Late that year I came on to see after it. By this time the move had attracted much attention and excited no little interest; and the day after I came, Mr. Middleton, then Clerk of the Court, said he desired very much to see the Southern lawyers back in court, and recommended me to get, if I could, Mr. Matt Carpenter, to appear in the case. I spoke to him and obtained his aid. The case was argued in that term, Johnson, Carpenter, R. H. Marr and myself appearing for it, and Mr. Speed, Attorney General, and the courtly and polished Stanbery, Special Counsel, against it. The Court held the case for some time under advisement, and then ordered a reargument, which was had; and in due time a decision by one majority was rendered in its favor."

The case won for A. H. Garland so much popularity that he was early in the next year, 1867, elected to the Senate without opposition, and appeared to take his seat on March 4, 1867; but was not permitted to do so, as Congress refused at that time to admit representatives from the South. The next few years he continued to practice law at Little Rock. His practice was vastly too much for one man to manage, and he was, at different times, associated both with General Sterling Cockrill and Colonel J. N. Smithee in law partnership. Mr. Garland was one of the Attorneys, in the Missouri Courts, in the greatest case that was ever decided by the United States Supreme Court, the case of Dred Scott.

* * * *

Before going into Mr. Garland's public career as Governor of Arkansas, it is necessary to briefly outline the events just preceeding, which are important in the history of the State, and in which Mr. Garland took an important part. The facts of history are taken from Shinn's History of Arkansas. Baxter was inaugurated governor January 6, 1873. He was a member of the minstrel wing of the Republican party, but had promised to administer the laws in the interest of the people, without regard to party. Brooks, his opponent, believed that the governorship was his, and contested the election of Mr. Baxter before the legislture, but without success. He then tried to get recognition before the United States Court, the Supreme Court, and, as a last resort, the Pulaski Circuit Court, but to no avail. In the meantime Baxter's acts did not please that wing of his party which had elected him, and it turned its forces over to declaring that he had not been rightfully elected. On the other hand, the Democrats, who had before opposed Baxter, turned now to his aid. Brooks repaired to the governor's office, and forcibly ejected him. He himself was sworn in May 15, 1874, and held office thirty days. In the meantime, Gov. Baxter drove out to St. John's College, and was there guarded from attack by two companies of cadets.

During the trying days just before the election of Baxter, he had a corps of advisors:—H. C. Caldwell, E. H. English, F. W. Compton, U. M. Rose, and Mr. Garland,—which, for courage, legal ability, and character, has never been surpassed. These called upon him at St. John's College, and the situation was discussed. A committee of prominent citizens did likewise, and all advised him to declare martial law, assuring him that the people thought his cause was just and would uphold it. After due deliberation he did so. The militia began pouring in from all sides, and Little Rock became the theatre of war. Men were honestly divided in this great contest, known in history as the Brooks-Baxter War, and the two opposing forces were led by two ex-Confederate soldiers, General Fagan and Colonel Newton. These matters were telegraphed to Washington, and both sides awaited the decision of Federal authorities. President Grand finally decided that the legislature of Arkansas was the body to decide the question. The legislature met on May 11, 1874, and decided that Baxter was the legal governor. On May 15, Grant issued his proclamation in favor of Baxter, and commanded Brooks and his followers to disperse, which they did.

The legislature passed an act calling a convention to frame a new constitution for the State. The convention met on July 14, and a new constitution removing all disfranchisements and registrations was framed, submitted to the people, and ratified by them.

As a return for the faithfulness of the Democratic leaders who had aided him, Mr. Baxter had determined to establish a government that would do away with the evils of carpet-bag government, and give the people their rights. He had therefore called the convention mentioned above. Many of the ablest men of the State were delegates to this convention, and they framed the Constitution under which the people of Arkansas now live. Under it almost every office is in the hands of the people, instead of being subject to the appointing power of the governor. By it the legislature, the cities, and the counties are forbidden to issue bonds or levy heavy taxes. Under it the people have gradually taken to themselves the decision of all political and economic questions, and gained the power of governing themselves with enterprise, economy and wisdom.

Governor Baxter ordered an election of officers under the new Constitution. He did this despite the fact that he would lose half his term, as he had been elected for four years and had served but two. He is said to have been urged to run for re-election for the governorship, but declined, saying that if he accepted the nomination, it would appear that he had done what he had in order to get the support of the Democrats. Mr. Garland was an earnest supporter of Mr. Baxter, and had zealously espoused his cause in the struggle. He had been appointed Deputy Secretary of State when Baxter was first elected. He perhaps had as much or more than any one else to do in laying the plans and directing the movements which resulted in restoring Governor Baxter to power. **And now,** when Baxter declined the race for re-election, the Democrats nominated Augustus H. Garland without opposition. In the general election he received 78,000 votes, against 24,000 for his opponent.

Very soon after Mr. Garland was inaugurated as governor, he was confronted by a proclamation made by Volney V. Smith, lieutenant-governor under Mr. Baxter, declaring himself the successor of Baxter and the rightful governor of Arkansas. This declaration was based upon the assertion that the acts of the legislature in calling a contitutional convention, etc., were null and void. Governor Garland ordered the arrest of Smith, and offered a reward for his apprehension. Smith wrote to President Grant protesting and asking for aid. Following is a copy of the letter, giving his point of view, obtained from Flemming's "Documentary History of Reconstruction:"

Little Rock, Nov. 16, 1874.

From Smith to President Grant:

The State government is completely overthrown by the connivance of Elisha Baxter, as that of Louisiana was by Penn's militia. It is true that the revolution by which it was accomplished was bloodless, but it was just as effectually done as though it had cost a thousand lives. Baxter himself used the office of Governor to organize the present revolutionary government. It was perfected in all its departments, civil and military, before he abdicated the office and turned over the same to Garland. When Baxter ceased to act, he yielded the office to a person who was the head of the new government, backed by a well-armed militia. In the face of such overwhelming advantages on the part of the Garland government, it would be worse than madness for me to try to re-establish the overthrown government by force of arms. It is because I am powerless that I appeal to you for aid. Before the life of any citizen is sacrificed, I desire to know from you, who are the arbiter between Garland and myself, whether I will be regarded as the rightful executive of a lawful government, or as being guilty of treason against it."

Representations were also made to President Grant early in 1875 that the Constitution of 1868 had been overthrown by violence, and a new one adopted. In a special message, he reported the matter to Congress. Governor Garland invited the committee, known as the Poland investigating committee, to visit Arkansas and investigate the matter from the beginning. The committee examined witnesses from the Democratic party and from both wings of the Republican party, and on February 19, 1875, reported to Congress that no interference with the existing government of Arkansas, by any department of the United States Government, was advisable. Congress adopted the report, and Arkansas escaped Federal interference with her local affairs. (From Shinn's History.) President Grant shortly afterward appointed Smith consul to the Island of St. Thomas, and he left Arkansas for that place.

To show the warm spirit in Arkansas at that time, a glowing account from the Fort Smith Herald, extra edition, is given:

FORT SMITH HERALD—EXTRA

Tuesday, Nov. 17, 1874.

78,000 against 24,000!

Trouble again! Baxter out! Garland in! Baxter's Lieutenant-Governor proclaims himself Governor.

78,000 people say that Garland is Governor.

It now remains for that 78,000 people to sustain Garland and the free voice of the people. Let the people be true to themselves. Let them come up like men, if needs be, and stand by their colors. The Garland government is the people's government. The lieutenant-governor and his Bourbon allies must be suppressed. If it be war, let it be war to the knife, and the knife to the hilt, if they force us to it, in defense of the new constitution, and the officers elected under it. Now is the time; and if Garland will have Smith and his followers arrested, tried and executed by drum-head court-maritial and shot; that done, go for

CLAYTON, DORSEY,

and their abettors. Then we will be rid of the great curse, and Arkansas will be free! Sic semper tyrannis!

Thus we see that Mr. Garland was chosen to be governor in a critical and turbulent period of his State's history. Feeling ran high when the carpet-bag government was overthrown, and there was a demand for the punishment of the leaders. But Gov. Garland began the pursuance of a broad and liberal policy. He allowed neither persecutions nor prosecutions. Taking the reins of government at the zenith of a successful revolution, when violence sought gratification, when passion struggled for the mastery, by a conservative policy, he soothed the one and discouraged the other. This policy he early announced in his first proclamation, as follows:—"Should there be any indictments in the courts for past political offenses, I would suggest and advise their dismissal. Let the people of all parties, races, and colors, come together, be welcomed to our State, and encouraged to bring her up to a position of true greatness."

The impoverished economical and financial condition of the State at the time of Mr. Garland's entrance upon the duties of office, was appalling. Resources were shattered, fortunes lost, and the people discouraged. Mr. Garland himself said that when he first went into office there was not enough money in the State treasury to buy the kindling necessary to start a fire in his office. But he went about everywhere inspiring hope in the people by his example of courage and fortitude in this trying time. He administered the government with so much tact that the wounds of the past were rapidly healed, and good feeling restored. He built up the financial interests of the State, and restored confidence everywhere. The State government was conducted for two months on the promissory notes of individuals, and after that on borrowed money, for which loans were effected, but which in time were all paid back and liquidated. The first loan of $200,000 was paid back in June, 1876. Expenditures were cut down, and an effort was made to keep them within the limits of the appropriations. It was naturally not long before the change for the better began to take place. Scrip began to rise in value and before many years was all redeemed and destroyed. Thus was Mr. Garland largely instrumental in restoring prosperity to Arkansas, and people began to rebuild their scattered and dilapidated fortunes, that had been placed in the pitiless scales of war.

So hopeful were the people that the legislature on November 30, 1875, made an appropriation to erect a building at the Centennial Exposition of the United States, to be held at Philadelphia the next year. The building was erected, and was an honor to the exhibition as well as to the State. The Bureau of Awards granted prizes to Arkansas:—(1) For a large, well-planned building; (2) For a large and attractive exhibit of the natural and industrial products of the State; (3) For a large collection of native woods; (4)

For an exhibit of agricultural products, especially of corn and cotton, the latter equalling any fibre of its kind in the United States. In addition the State took other prizes. This was the first effort of that common wealth to display her resources, and did much to allay sectional feeling and reunite the people.

SECTION II

The above is the important mission which Mr. Garland had to fill as governor of his State. The people, never ungrateful to a benefactor and a statesman, were ready to give him "higher things," and in 1877 he was elected without opposition to succeed Powell Clayton in the Senate of the United States. And this time he was admitted to that assembly—the arena where his fame, already having travelled across the nation, was to be maintained and increased, and where he was to restore the glory of former days, when Arkansas was represented in the Senate by Ashley and Sevier. At the expiration of his first term, he was re-elected with practically no opposition. Of the pages that are to follow dealing with his senatorial career, there needs must be some words of introduction. Any report of his utterances in that Chamber must necessarily be imperfect and incomplete. Many of his speeches are not mentioned for want of space. Several are herewith quoted almost in full—the most important—and quotations and notes are made from many others. But they are all upon the Congressional Record, which is the source of information of this search, and the authority for the facts here stated. His speeches should prove a constant pride to every patriotic citizen of Arkansas. The quotations that are made, unless they be from speeches on issues of great national

---

The references are all given by dates instead of by the method, Cong. Rec. 42 Cong., 1 Sess. p. 101, (for instance) As the dates appear on the backs of the volumes of Cong. Rec., the speeches may be found just as easily in this way.

importance, are selected mainly for two reasons: first, to show certain characteristics of the man; and second, to show their importance or meaning to the State of Arkansas. Some selected for the latter reason should be of more special interest to those who live in that State.

Mr. Garland first entered the Senate of the United States at the opening of the session of 1877-8, early in December, 1877. He was honored by being placed upon the Standing Senate committees on Public Lands and on Territories, December 6. Of course he took but little part in the debate during his first session. On December 11, he had a bill read twice to establish a certain post-route in Arkansas. It was referred to the committee on Post-offices and Post-roads, but got no further.

On February 18, 1878, he submitted the following resolution, which was considered by unanimous consent and agreed to: "Resolved, that the Secretary of War be requested to make a report to the Senate of the work of removing a certain bar in the Arkansas river near Fort Smith; whether any further appropriation is needed to successfully complete the same, and if so, what amount."

On May 1, Mr. Garland introduced a bill authorizing the appointment of a committee of three Senators, three Congressmen, and three others not members of either House, to inquire:—

(1)—Into the relative effects of the tariff under the existing law upon the different industries of the country.

(2)—Into the relative effects of the existing tariff upon the consumer and producer.

(3) Into the relative merits of the specific and ad valorem system.

(4)—What, if any, improper discriminations exist under the present law.

(5)—What changes are necessary to be made to insure a wholesome law on the tariff, etc.

(6)—Into, and review the whole tariff system, as now existing.

(7)—That the said commission report the result of their examination, with recommendations, at the earliest possible time.

This bill was read a second time by its title, and referred to the Committee on Finance. This concludes his work in the Senate for the first term. He could not be expected to have spoken much then, because he would thereby have broken in upon that precedent of Senatorial dignity, which means that new Senators, for sometime after arrival, "be seen and not heard."

Mr. Garland was back at the opening of Congress, December 3, 1878, and was again appointed on the standing committee on Public Lands and on Territories, and also was appointed on the special committee of December 4, for the Prevention of Epidemic Diseases.

On December 5, he made a few remarks which show in a manner his idea of the individual's relation to the government. The facts were:—Geo. W. Clarke, of Crawford County, Ark., was appointed Indian agent, and gave bonds for such, in 1854. Jesse Warner and others went on his bond as sureties. All who were worth the amount claimed were dead at this time, except Warner. Clarke was found to be in default, and relieved from duty in 1856. Those who went on his bond were notified in 1875. Warner, the only living one, sued to be relieved from liability. The investigating committee believed that great injustice had been done to the sureties by the delay on the part of the Government, and thought that they should be relieved from liability on the bond. Mr. Garland held to this opinion, and he said:—

"A high and lofty consideration lies at the bottom of this matter. It is said that no government is bound by statute unless specially barred. But when the government puts herself in the position of an individual and goes into the courts of the country, she is held to the same degree of diligence, and the same exercise of energy, to which the individual is held. Her rights stand no better and no higher in that tribunal, than those of the individual who attends before it. Many of the sureties have died, and but one now, in Arkansas, is worth the money claimed on the bond. He is a high and respectable attorney of that State, and advanced in years. His application speaks in louder and better words than I can speak. I am always prepared to do right in a given case presented to me; and you may bring cases of this kind as often as you please, at every turn of the clock in the day, if you please, and I shall vote for them, come from what section of the country they may."

On December 12, certain Senators got into a wrangle over a bill claiming to protect the Hot Springs Reservation at Hot Springs, Ark., from the encroachments of individual's building houses over the springs, and thus controlling the water from them. Mr. Garland said, in answer to a speech made by Mr. Hill, of Georgia:—

"The point of Mr. Hill was, to protect the indigent and the poor people, that they may have the full use of the hot water. In that I fully concur. But there is a clause in the bill itself providing for free baths for the use of the indigent. No one big iron bath-house can procure a lease so as to infringe on this right. The bill provides that the government shall lease the grounds on which the Arlington Hotel stands, to its proprietors, and also to give to owners of bath-houses the sites on which their houses stand. The question of the title to Hot Springs has been in the courts for over thirty years, the government holding all the time the fee, never having issued the patent to anybody. In 1870 Congress passed the statute compelling parties to go before the Court of Claims and litigate with the United States the right to this property. Have the parties, to whom leases have been already made no rights in equity, and should they not be considered in adjusting these matters? This is but a temporary provision to enable these parties to have their titles adjusted there. I am committed to none. I am as free and independent as to my actions toward that property, after the rights of my constituents there are determined, as if the property were in Pensacola or in Brooklyn. Leases have been made under the color of law, and the question is, shall we ignore and trample them under foot? There is great necessity for enacting the bill. It is almost a land without law there. It is time that Congress was doing something. The various propositions for the government to build hotels, lease bath-houses, etc., can come up at the proper time. So far as I represent the State of Arkansas, I am committed to none of them."

On February 5, 1879, the discussion of the thirteenth, fourteenth and fifteenth amendments to the Constitution was up, and Mr. Garland spoke at considerable length. He offered an amendment to the resolution of Senator Morgan, of Alabama, offered as a substitute for the resolution of Senator Edmunds of Vermont. Garland's amendment inserted after "that" the word "although," and inserted also, "were not adopted in a legal manner," etc., to the words "are as," etc., making it read: "Resolved, that although the thirteenth, fourteenth and fifteenth amendments to the constitu-

tion of the United States were not adopted in a legal
manner, yet having been accepted, recognized, and
acquiesced in by the States, they are as valid and bind-
ing as any other part of the Constitution; that the people of the United States have a common interest in the
enforcement of the whole Constitution in every State
and Territory; and that it's alike the right and duty
of the United States, so far as the power has been delegated to them, to enforce said amendments, and to protect every citizen in the exercise of all the rights thereby secured." Although Mr. Garland's amendment
received but five votes—Garland, Beck, Harris,
McDonald and Vorhees—yet no one of the opposition
for one moment doubted his sincerity of purpose or
earnestness of effort; and even they, in their speeches,
paid him the highest tributes, not merely in a formal
and polite manner, but out of warm respect and regard.
Owing to its importance as showing Mr. Garland's
views of the amendments, the greater part of his
remarks is herewith given:—

"There is a difference between these three amendments and the other amendments to the Constitution.
It is to draw this distinction that my amendment to
the resolution is made. It is drawn in plain language.
I could have said, instead of 'legal manner,' 'in due
form,' or 'in due process of law,' but the good old word,
'manner' is understood better in the country—in the
midst of the people who have to bear the taxes and
burdens of the government. When the amendments
were adopted, eleven of the States of the Union had no
representation here. Upon these States they were to
operate, as well as on the others. The farce, which
amounted later to a tragedy, was gone through, of
submitting them to those States for ratification.
Whether you indulge in the theory of what is called
States Rights, or liberal construction, we must not

forget, nor can any of us ever forget, that it is the people at last who compose the government. When they had not an opportunity to speak on the amendments, it is little more than a farce to say that they have been adopted by the States in a government made, carried on, and conducted by the people. My people had no more voice in the adoption of the amendments than if they had lived in Peru. Three-fourths of the people in Arkansas were disfranchised. The question was never submitted to the people. The legislatures were elected irrespertive of these questions; and they in some instances represented no person this side of the moon. The fact that the Secretary of State promulgated the amendments does not help the case, because he was simply announcing to the country what already had been passed, and which in reality had never been voted on by all the people. The thirteenth and fourteenth amendments, and especially the former, came while the South was in the very throes of war. The fifteenth came when three-fourths were disfranchised.

"But while I religiously and conscientiously believe that under the law and the Constitution of this country they were not attended with the least legality in their ratification, yet they are as firmly and fixedly a part of the Constitution as any other of the amendments. The States, ever since they have been restored to their integrity, have accepted and recognized them. As Governor of Arkansas, I got the legislature to legislate directly and indirectly on these amendments. They are enforced in that State, and there is not a man in Arkansas, so far as I know, to whatever party he belongs, who would escape from them.

"I do not accept the decisions of the Supreme Court, acting here in my legal capacity, merely because they are such. I must be left to judge of the Constitution, in all of its parts, upon my own judgment, and I must take the responsibility of that judgment, whether it be good, bad, or indifferent."

A little later in the discussion, Mr. Garland, said:—

"The amendment is offered in good faith and as one of the convictions of my soul after a very long and painful examination of this question in more years than one. I take the responsibility of any error I may have made. I believe that even in the United States Senate, a man ought to express his honest convictions when he expresses any. The amendment is upon the record with my remarks. I will invite the Senate to a vote on it, and if it gets no other vote than my own, it shall receive that. I have no terror of being in the minority, for I have been the greater part of my life in the minority. I stated in my remarks before that I had enforced these amendments (in Arkansas), for the purpose of showing that they are valid; but that they were valid through any legal process of ratification there is not power enough in this world or the next to make me say, in this or any other tribunal. But with all the detestation that I have for the origination of these amendments, I will never agree that any joint resolution of these two Houses of Congress shall repeal them. They have now been recognized by legislation of the Southern States, and are parts of the Constitution."

Mr. Garland's tribute to Jefferson Davis was delivered in the Senate May 1, 1879. The bill was up, providing "that the law granting pensions to the soldiers and their widows of the War of 1812, be made applicable in all its provisions to the soldiers and sailors who served in the war with Mexico of 1846." To this a proviso was made by Senator Hoar of Massachusetts, "that no pension shall ever be paid under this act to Jefferson Davis, the late President of the 'so-called' Confederacy." This naturally aroused considerable resentment on the part of Senators from the South. The words of Mr. Garland quoted here are in no sense given because of any sectional feeling they may convey. He said:—

"So far as Mr. Davis is concerned, I do not suppose he wants a pension, or ever thought of it for a moment. As one who served with him in a civil capacity in the late war (in the Confederate Congress), I wish I had the power and the authority now, and I know it would accord with every impulse of his heart, to enter here upon the record before the people of the country, a receipt in full to the Senator from Massachusetts, and all others who hold his views toward that distinguished gentleman. He would scorn it if tendered grudgingly. He was a gallant soldier in the Mexican War. His services are on the record of his country, and while they may not surpass, yet they will equal in history, all Grecian fame and all Roman glory. Mr. Davis while he would be proud of any recognition of his services for his country at any time, yet if he believed there was a man, woman or child in Massachusetts who begrudged him recognition, he would scorn it and turn from it as he would turn from the hiss of an adder.

"Mr. Davis and myself were not in a general way of the same politics in reference to this government; but I have never had occasion, in the long service that I had with him and under him, in a civil capacity entirely, to doubt his capacity, his integrity, or power of purpose under any and all circumstances; and I will say to the Senator from Massachusetts, and all others who agree with him, that whenever they seek to see a game man die, whether in adversity or prosperity, they may go to the dying bed of Jefferson Davis, and they will witness that fact.

"He is a bold man, indeed, who would say that this government has not been generous to those they con-

quered; but he is a much bolder man who would say
that they have been generous. I deny that the conduct
of the government toward Davis has been generous.
When he was incarcerated in the prisons of 'their country,' as they called it, poor and emaciated and broken
down, beyond the power of doing harm to any living
person, much less to any living government, and carried to Richmond almost as often as Troy viewed her
walls encircled and her chief pursued, to stand his trial,
they dared not try him and they have not to this day
tried him. The sacred right of trial has been denied
him, though he has sought and implored it, from time
to time, and his attorneys for him. How could he, in
decency's name, in the name of all that is worth pleading for, ask the country to pardon him, when they kept
him in chains, although liberated upon the bond of
friends in the North? The conduct, instead of being
generous, has been cruel; it is barbarous, it is inhuman.

"I look about and see others who served in the
Mexican War honored by the government. Yet Jefferson Davis cannot receive a pittance from the government he has served so well, and the mere mention
of it stirs the blood of gentlemen who talk of generosity to indignation. You talk of generosity and you
speak of the proud eras of your history. Why, sir,
in the proudest era of Roman History, no general was
ever permitted to have a triumph or bear a trophy
that he had won in a civil war; and the produest and
greatest military nation of modern Europe, England,
has had her escutcheon blurred because she held the
great Napoleon a prisoner, as this Government would
have held Jefferson Davis, but for the generosity of
Horace Greely and a few others, the latchets of whose
political shoes those who are urging this motion are
unworthy to unloose."

At the opening of the session of 1879-80, Mr. Garland was appointed on the Judiciary Committee, and made Chairman of the Committee on Territories. He was also appointed on three out of the eight special committees. On January 21, 1880, he was appointed on the Senatorial Board of visitors to attend the next annual examination of the Cadets at the United States Military Academy at West Point. He re-introduced his bill providing for a commission to examine into the subject of the tariff, with a view to facilitating legislation thereto. It was again referred to the Committee on Finance, but got no further. He also introduced, among others, a bill (Senate bill No. 925) to provide for the reappraisement of the abandoned military reservation at Fort Smith, Ark. This was referred to the Committee on Public Lands, but got no further.

On December 18 a bill was up providing that a committee of five be appointed, which should obtain information of methods which would lead to the emigration of negroes northward. Mr. Garland humorously referred to his own State: "From the leading colored gentlemen of Arkansas, I have letters informing me that but few have ever left that State, and those few have returned to take up their abode again; consistent with the saying that no man ever left that State yet, white or black, who did not go back there to live again, except one poor individual who sickened while manfully making his way back, and died before he could reach the confines of his State."

On March 18, Mr. Garland made a long speech, or series of speeches, in the debate on the bills for the establishment of titles at Hot Springs (H. R. Bill No. 4244), upon which he had spoken brieby on December 12, 1878. He had time and time again sought the Senate and begged it to take up this matter and vote upon it, before the session should end. But they had hesitated and neglected it. Mr. Garland's speech was very long.

He went into the elaborate details of the case. He
argued that the people at Hot Springs had practically
made the land's value, by their own improvements
upon it; and that, while it was a large matter finan-
cially to those people, many of whom had been born
to believe that they had as good a right to the property as to the clothes upon their backs, it was a mere
pittance to the government. Nobody would be taxed
to pay it; no person would lose by it. The government
would have several thousand dollars surplus from the
property after giving these persons the little bit which
the bill proposed. It was, he said, an important matter
to them, but a mere drop in the bucket to the government. He said:—"The State of Arkansas is not asking for the lands; but citizens of Arkansas come to you
asking you for this favor or gratuity, and many persons from various States of the Union. Hot Springs
is now the most cosmopolitan city of its size in the
world. I ask the Senate in all sincerity if this is exorbitant, if this is an outrage either on justice or fairness, when you are trying to deal out equity to these
people? I have more reason probably than any other
man in public life to desire that there should be an end
to the litigation of this trouble. For eighteen years,
long before I was in the Senate, I was connected with
the litigation in reference to Hot Springs, and I know
every foot of this land. The place itself I love, and
there I believe I am loved; indeed this ground is my
second home. Hence this feeling I manifest upon the
subject." And the bill was passed.

On March 23, the bill providing for the distribu-
tion of the Geneva Award fund was up for consideration, upon which Mr. Garland spoke at considerable
length. The act of 1874 had disposed of part of this
fund, but there was a balance of nine and one-half
million dollars left, and the question was, what should

be done with that? Mr. Garland thought that when the facts were known as to how the United States got hold of this fund, they would be legally compelled to distribute it in a certain way. The money came to the Treasury as the result of the want of exercise of due diligence on the part of Great Britain in preventing Confederate Cruisers from arming themselves and departing from her ports, and committing depredations on the property of the United States and its citizens. There was a dispute on this point between the United States and Great Britain. In order to settle it amicably and not go to war, it was determined to settle the matter by arbitration. A commission was appointed for this purpose, which sat at Geneva. The commission met under certain hard and fast rules, which were to bind its conduct. The government made claims before the commission for destruction of her vessels and property, etc.; and also private claims, for destruction of those belonging to individuals. Now the counsel for the United States wished the Commission to pay her the indemnity fund, out of which she should distribute shares to her individual citizens who had suffered.

Mr. Garland held that the United States received indemnity not for the benefit of the American government, as such, but for her citizens, as trustees for those citizens. This excluded everything except payment for direct losses or destruction of vessels and their cargoes by those cruisers (the Florida, Alabama, and Shenandoah). The commission simply gave to the government a lump sum for individual losses, to be distributed by it, and including also the government losses, where the government had any proprietary interest in ships destroyed by the inculpated cruisers. We quote, in part, from Mr. Garland's remarks:—

"I do not know, so far as I am concerned, what bet-

ter business the general government can be at than
protecting her individual citizens who pay her taxes
and fight her battles for her. I am not willing to write
myself down for one as consenting to the doctrine that
this government affords no protection to those people,
simply because they have not a strictly legal right or a
technical legal remedy. We cannot shelter ourselves
behind the idea that the government cannot become an
agent, a trustee. Has not Congress established a
Court of Claims, in which an individual can sue the
government?

"The simple question now is, shall the fund be distributed to the losers of those vessels and cargoes, and
those persons who paid insurance thereon? This is the
legal question. Now, will Congress execute the legal
right, or will it set itself up to take in the unexplored
field of charity or mercy, to find some object worthy of
the bestowal of the fund? To pay just those who have
a legal right, and if there is a surplus give that to those
who suffered in consequence of the depredations of
those cruisers, if you can get at them, is right.

"We have seen what high hopes have been placed in
the commission at Geneva in the interests of peace to
the civilized world. If this Congress or any other Congress disregards the arbitration, and says, 'We will distribute this fund as we see proper, outside the compress of the award,' this splendid hope and bright
vision are gone forever, and we shall never have
another international arbitration to settle the disputes
of this kind. If the bill is not correct upon its merits
and general principles, we have no right to this money
at all, and had better send it back to England, for we
hold it under false pretense."

Mr. Garland spoke at other times when this bill was
up again, and we quote again below from his further
arguments on the subject. We do not quote it here,

as it came in a later session of Congress, and would spoil the chronological order in which we are placing his speeches.

On the bill "making appropriations to supply certain deficiencies in the appropriations for the services of the government for the year ending June 30, 1880," Mr. Garland spoke briefly on March 31, saying that Arkansas was deeply interested in the matter. The only complaint he had against the bill was that the amount it proposed was insufficient. Much money, he said was needed to clear out the swamps of Arkansas. The Swamps Land Act of September 28, 1880, granted swamp lands to the States. In perfecting these gifts the question had arisen as to what lands were swamp. He said that these disputes were unsettled, and many valuable lands were held up, their titles in abeyance, for want of adjustment. The appropriation of $6,000,-000, provided by the bill, was, he said, insufficient to complete the work. Let the government go forward manfully and settle these disputes.

Mr. Garland, it will be remembered, had, two years before, introduced a bill providing that a commission be appointed to look into the matter of the tariff, and report to the Senate. He first spoke on the subject May 27, 1880. He had introduced the bill, he said, simply to get more accurate information about the then existing tariff; how, if at all, it was unfit in its operation, and wherein it could be revised so as to cure these bad results. Complaints had been made that whatever law there was on the subject had not been enforced in its true spirit and meaning. Complaints were also made that the tariff system had been burdensome in the way of expense to the government. Mr. Garland said that the government had absolutely groaned under it. The existing tariff was enacted, he said, to defray the expenses of the war, and was a tariff springing from a spirit of retaliation, and not based upon justice. Every one argued that some tariff suitable to the interests of the country, and properly adjusted to them, should be adapted at the earliest possible time. It was to get such a movement on foot that he had introduced the bill, and he made speeches later on the tariff which, from the array of figures and facts presented, must have consumed much valuable time in their preparation.

A case showing how vigorously Mr. Garland stood up for his constituents at home, came up on June 12. Under the bill (H. R. No. 6325) "making appropriations to supply deficiencies in the appropriations for the fiscal year ending June 30, 1880, and for prior years, and for other purposes," he made a resolution to pay Jas. F. Fagen, late marshal of the Western District of Arkansas $2,116.27, the amount found to be due him as such marshal, at a trial had in the district court for the western district of Arkansas in 1879, in a suit by the United States on his official bond as such marshal. Fagan was marshal under the appointment of General Grant, and after his term of office expired the government instituted a suit in the district court on his official bond, for an amount alleged to be due to the United States, which Fagan had failed to pay over. Fagan appeared in the suit, and plead, among other things, an offset. After a long and exhaustive trial it was obtained by the verdict of the jury, that, instead of Fagan owing the United States, the latter owed him the sum stated, on his transaction as marshal.

But of course no judgment could be recovered against the United States for this money. A jury can find that the government owes money, but no court can render judgment upon the finding, except the Court of Claims, unless there be a special act conferring jurisdiction for that purpose. "As a matter of course," said Mr. Garland, "it is not a judgment against the government, but it is a finding that it is that much in default to Fagan, and the whole matter is transferred to Congress for its disposal as it sees proper. You have the verdict of twelve men. There are only two ways that Fagan can get his money; either through an appropriation by Congress, or by having a special bill passed to send him to the Court of Claims, and put him through that tribunal, involving a delay of two or three years, and the cost of lawyers' fees, etc. Which will Congress do? It must appropriate the money now, or it must compel him to present a bill for his special relief, and have it referred to the Committee on Claims to make him go through that process, or send him under a special act to the court of Claims. I have presented my resolution to the Senate. I do not want Mr. Fagan submitted to the process of coming here with a bill for his special relief and having the matter re-investigated, or to go to the Court of Claims and spend all his money to employ lawyers." And Mr. Garland's resolution was passed.

In the next session of Congress, December, 1880 to March, 1881, Mr. Garland got a bill through Congress (S. Bill No. 711) "amending the charter of the Freedman's Savings and Trust Company, and for other purposes." The bill was reported to the Special Committee on the Freedman's Savings and Trust Co., recommitted, reported back with an amendment, the amendment agreed to, and the bill passed by the Senate; received, considered and passed by the House, examined and signed, and approved by the President. He also submitted the following resolution, among many others, which was unanimously considered and agreed to:—
"That the committee on Military Affairs be instructed to inquire whether the United States arsenal buildings

and grounds at Little Rock, Ark., be not one of the forts "of but slight value for military purposes," owing to the changed condition of the country, and the operation of which is continued at great expense to the country, referred to in the President's last message; and if the same cannot with proper regard to the service, be disposed of to Arkansas, and if so, upon what terms."

Mr. Garland's attitude on the question of pensions is shown in a few well-chosen words, spoken on December 9. He said: "I stand here prepared in every instance to vote for an application for pension by a husband, unless it is shown that he had made on his part an expressed renunciation of the claim for it; and I am not so sure but that in cases of that sort I should vote for his widow to get it, when he dies and she desires it; because these pensions are given somewhat in the nature of a homestead right, and cannot be waived by the head of the family, the original party, but must be retained for the benefit of those who came after him. The case is none the less worthy, none the less meritorious because the husband failed to make the application himself. The matter of pensions is at least one of generosity, while to some extent it is one of justice. It is not a fixed and unyielding and unbending rule, that because a person, under the existing pension laws, is not entitled to a fee, therefore Congress should not give it to him. Congress is the great repository of the power, and should exercise it with the utmost liberality, to those who claim as the widow in this case does."

Mr. Garland spoke briefly, on December 6, on the bill to establish an educational fund, and apply a portion of the proceeds of the public lands to public education. He said:—"The system of aiding common schools by the government has been ingrafted in every conceivable plan of legislation, even antedating the Constitution itself. From the splendid opinion of Judge Campbell in the case of Cooper vs. Robinson, there never has been a doubt of the power of the government to aid, foster, and do all that it can for the public schools. Congress has given lands to the States for internal improvements. Certainly it has the right to appropriate them, or their proceeds, for the highest of all objects, the education of its citizens. Congress has the power in the constitution; we have judicial decisions; we have the precedent of legislation. The very best institution we have ever had in my state, the Industrial University at Fayetteville, which is now an ornament to the State and country, owes its birth, and in great part its growth, to the act of 1862. Arkansas lays a tax, a liberal one in her impoverished condition; and we have a good and promising system of free schools. The passage of the bill will prove a great help to her."

But Mr. Garland did not believe that this fund should be given directly to the States; and he spoke against amendment to that effect. He argued that if the money be given directly in lump to the States, it would become mixed up in State politics, and instead of being a benefit bestowed, it would be an evil. There would be no limitations, with no one to account to, as to how the fund should be distributed. "The benefit immediately from this bill," he said, "will be small. No school-house will be built upon every hill-top in Arkansas and other states. We cannot at once take care of the great mass of ignorance thrown upon this country so suddenly by the war, but we propose to lay a foundation, by which after a while, as certainly as the needle points to the pole, we may redeem this ignorance in the South and in other portions of the country. We may heal it, but not by giving the fund directly."

Mr. Garland was very fond of using humorous illustrations, and employed them very often for emphasis. A case of this kind was the conclusion of his speech on the bill providing that a man named Ben Holladay "be authorized to institute and prosecute an action in the Court of Claims against the United States, for the recovery of an amount of any seizure or destruction by hostile Indians of property owned by him and used in performing his contract with the government to transport the mails on the then overland mail route between the Missouri river and Salt Lake City, from 1868 to November 3, 1876." Mr. Garland favored the bill in eloquent terms and with clear reasoning, consuming considerable time in speaking. He said he knew little or nothing of Holladay, but favored the bill because he thought it just. He considered it the first great duty of the government to do justice to its citizens, and not keep them there asking for compensation, sending them from one court to another. He finished by telling of a man from Arkansas, named Ray, who was in Washington with a claim of $2,500 for the destruction of a steamboat, in the war, on the lower Red river, at the time when he (Garland) was there seeking his pardon from President Johnson. Ray thought he would get his money in a few days. Six years after Garland came back to the Supreme Court and Ray was still waiting. Six years after that Garland was sent to the Senate, and Ray was there on the same spot where he had left him six years before. Garland said:—"How are you, Ray? Have you got your claim?" "No," was the answer, "but I think I'll get it in a few days." After about two years Ray did get his claim, and when he paid his lawyer's fees and hotel bills he had $300.00 left. Mr. Garland said that this was an actual fact.

Another case showing the great man's humorous nature took place on February 10. Mr. Pugh, of Alabama, had made a long and able presentation of facts and reasons favoring the expenditure of $1,000,000, under the direction of the Postmaster General, in the establishment of mail steamship lines, to be distributed among the Atlantic, Gulf, Mexican and Pacific ports. Mr. Garland had intended to speak on it, but after Mr. Pugh's speech he arose and said:—"The masterly presentation of the case to which we have just listened relieves me of the necessity of saying anything at all. I could not add anything. I simply point to the speech as the man did who had a prayer copied at the head of his bed, so as to save time, simply saying, when he went to bed, 'Lord, those are my sentiments.'"

In the special session of March 4 to May 20 and October 10 to October 29, 1881, Mr. Garland was again appointed on the committees on the Judiciary and on Territories, and also on the select committee on Epidemic Diseases.

A speech showing Mr. Garland's love and appeal for principle above politics, and right and justice above party lines, is given almost in full. The special session had been called by President Hayes, President Garfield delivered his inaugural address, etc. On March 24 the question of electing new officers—Secretary, Sergeant-at-Arms, Door-keeper, Chief Clerk, Principle Executive Clerk, and Chaplain, was up for discussion. The Republicans had gone so far as to assume the right of electing new officers, or re-organizing the Senate for a special Executive Session, just as is done at the beginning of a new session; and had presented names for these officers to the other side of the House for consideration. The right was by that side disputed. The Republicans held that the question of changing the officers was not a problem of the efficiency or ineffi-

ciency of the existing officers, but whether they (the
Republicans) had the numerical strength to change
them; and claimed that if they had this power they
also had the right to do it. Mr. Garland said:—

"As to the procedure that is asked for here of electing new officers for the Senate, my impression is that
it has not been the custom of the Senate to change its
officers at executive session. It has done so at extra
sessions of Congress; but the existing officers at the
close of a Congress have always continued through an
executive session following it.

"But I wish to speak to the Senate of what goes
beyond and above the mere question of party power or
party success. Until last Monday a week ago there
were not half a dozen men on the face of the earth
who knew for a certainty what the complexion of the
Senate would be on casting its vote on any proposition.
Upon the revealing of that fact I have nothing to say.
These are matters that gentlemen must take care of for
themselves, with a proper regard for their constituency and their accountability to them. The mixtures
and intermixtures of political bedfellows are like the
verdicts of petit-jurors, among the unaccountable
things—and life is too short for me to undertake now a
diagnosis of the matter. But there is the fact before
us that a number of gentlemen, officials of this Senate,
who are acceptable, against none of whom can a sin-
gle charge be brought, either of malfeasance of misfeas-
ance or of non-feasance in office, upon a sudden, not
even a respectable justice of the peace's notice, are
called upon to take up their beds and walk, without a
day's preparation, without a moments notice compared
with what should be given them. These gentlemen have
been here now nearly two years, some of them depend-
ing for nearly every particle of bread that they get
upon their small salary which they receive here; and

The Hubbard Residence—Washington, Ark.

they are called upon suddenly to leave, without any-where to go, like the Son of Man, who, as it was said in the Scriptures, hath not where to lay his head.

"I appeal to both sides of this Chamber. I am not speaking for party now at all, but I am speaking for these gentlemen who have demeaned themselves as faithful servants. Do not inflict an injury on these gentlemen—and probably an irreparable injury—for life. It is a matter of but a few days at best; and if an extra session of Congress is called, (which God in His wisdom forbid as one of the calamities to the country), you may then go forward and elect your officers, but now you will strike down some of the best officials the country has ever had, for a little gain of possibly a week or two, or a few months at most. It is not, seriously, my brother Senators, a subject worthy of your consideration. Let us see if there is not something decent and respectable at least, irrespective of party discipline or party whip, where we may meet together on a common ground and let this matter go over until the regular session. I do not wish to be drawn into a contest of this sort here, I do not, for the sake of the country, for the sake of all parties, desire it; and I ask you in the name of justice to these gentlemen who have had this short notice, to spare them a little more time. It is not simply because you have the numerical power that you have the right and should exercise it.

> " 'Oh! 'tis excellent
> To have a giant's strength; but tyrannous
> To use it like a giant.' "

At the session of 1881-2, Mr. Garland was retained on the standing committees on the Judiciary and on Territories, and on the special committee on Epidemic Diseases; and was appointed as a conferree on the bill

(H. R. 4166) to divide Iowa into judicial districts. During this session he got a bill through Congress (S. Bill No. 219) entitled "a bill for the relief of Rebecca Wright, widow of James Wright, a soldier in the War of 1812." He introduced many other bills, and mostly for the relief of certain people in his State. Many of them got through the Senate and to the House and some got no further than the committees to which they were entrusted for report. Besides these, he presented many petitions from people of Arkansas, some of which are: From citizens of Arkansas, for relief to sufferers from the overflow of the Mississippi; from Joseph Cossart and others of Clark County, praying for an appropriation for improvements on the Ouachita river in Arkansas; from citizens of Drew County, for aid to Education; from citizens of Eureka Springs, for the erecting of a hospital there; from citizens of Fort Smith, for the donation by the government of the military reservation there, for school purposes; from citizens of Little Rock, for the improvement of the Arkansas river; for a liberal improvement of the Hot Springs Reservation; from the Arkansas W. C. T. U. for General Prohibition; and from the Hot Springs Woman's Library Association, to erect a building. Nearly all of the bills which he introduced also had reference to the good of his State.

On December 12, 1881, Mr. Garland was up again speaking on the tariff, and he again spoke at great length. The matter, as was cited above, was before the Senate on May 20, 1880, and even as early as May 1878, when Mr. Garland first entered that body. Owing to the importance of the question of revising the tariff at that time, and as showing Mr. Garland's attitude on that great national issue, his speech is herewith given, in part:—

"The schedule of the present tariff, its confused

terms of law, the codification of the laws, the digest, the decision thereupon, together with the importance of the subject-matter of the revenue itself—these combine to show, outside of the reasons formerly adduced, the necessity for some kind of action.

"The Constitution provides that the House shall originate bills for revenue. But the notion of protection always comes, whether directly or indirectly, as a tail to that feature in the Constitution referring to revenue.

"A tariff, when fairly and justly levied, has always been a favorite way of raising revenue. But when a citizen is called upon to pay tax to the government, it should be in proportion to the ability of the citizen to pay. This maxim is violated in every tariff act which is originated for protection.

"I do not want absolute free trade. Some authors and public speakers claim that this will be the doctrine of all countries. So it is with the millenium or any other good time, when those animals we read of in the Bible shall lie down together and there shall be war no more. But as a practical question, there is no party favoring absolute free trade.

"As a matter of course, in the collection of revenue, under a wise and proper dispensation, the protection which follows must necessarily be allowed. There must be a margin for it: there is no question on that point. The exercising of many powers given in bulk to the Constitution carries with it incidents which are unavoidable, though not expressly granted. Neither the doctrine of protection, per se, nor free trade, has a resting place in this country, in my judgment; but the proper medium is to rest between the two, in the exercise of the revenue power by Congress; by a 'judicious system of tariff,' as General Jackson termed it.

"A system of protection leads to monopolies, and

such as are now pressing on this country beyond all powers combined, to its detriment and its injury. It may be covert; it may be secret; but it steps and marches to that as certainly as water will seek its level.

"We should have a consistant tariff law, we should have our tariff suit of clothes cut down more properly to our dimensions at this time, rather than wear them as they were ten or fifteen years ago. I want the whole system revised and placed in a compact and digestible form, so that it may show itself when it is read and examined.

"I am not ready to agree that the ever-present prosperity is due to the protective tariff. I have great reason to doubt, if not to deny it. Nearly everyone who has a hobby is willing to attribute prosperity to it. The country has lived and always will live, in spite of all this legislation."

Again, on March 23, 1882, Mr. Garland said:—"I never could see, in my reading and understanding of the Constitution, how Congress could proceed to collect a tax except for revenue to meet the exigencies of the government. I believe as sincerely as I believe anything that a connected argument upon that subject, from the first breath of Hamilton, on through Madison, down to the present time, taking all the public men of the past, could be established beyond any question, to show that the sole and only power is to levy that tax or tariff, and that revenue is the sole and only purpose of its levying. It is for revenue, and for revenue only—the present tariff was made as a war measure for the purposes of war, and necessarily had to be unjustly discriminating toward certain industries and interests."

Mr. Garland again advocated a mixed commission to examine the tariff, composed of members of the Senate and House, with three outsiders, making nine in all.

His purpose was that, when the results of the investigation should be returned to Congress, there would be some gentlemen on the floor of each House already trained to explain it to the others. The aim, he thought, ought to be to prevent the government from fostering any enterprises with which she has no national, no federal, concern. It was for the sake of improving private conditions and private fortunes. However, his amendment as to the way the commission should be made up was lost by a small majority of votes.

On February 9, Mr. Garland spoke again on the subject of pensions, giving still clearer statements than those in the speech on the subject, quoted from above. This time he spoke on the resolution declaratory against the repeal of the "Arrears of Pensions" Act. He said, in part:—

"This resolution is a plain common-sense statement of the proposition that if soldiers establish their claims to pensions, the pensions shall run from the time when their right or cause of action accrued, and that they shall not be compelled to wait until their children and their children's children are old and infirm before they receive their pensions. This is of course a just statute. I do not think Congress can seriously contemplate the repeal of this law on account of the great expense to the government, or on account of frauds occasioned by many persons getting pensions who do not deserve them. If the right to the pension exists, it is not worth while to talk of the cost, and especially since on all sides it is admitted that we are fully able to meet the expense. If frauds exist, let us try to find and weed them out.

"Our Civil War certainly grew into one of gigantic proportions, and became a public war, and controlled by the principle of public wars. The Supreme Court has constantly held that it was a war in which the existence of a country was at stake, and was to be considered in principle as if it had been carried on against Great Britain, France, and other powers combined. These soldiers, going into battle to gamble their lives away against balls of fire, saved the country—a country of which all of our are citizens united at this time; and the glory and prowess of these soldiers are the glory and prowess of all parts of the land; and as one of the vanquished, as one of those who went down in that conflict, I am not ashamed to acknowledge the propriety of voting these pensions. If they were the victors over us, I yield because I believe no other power on earth could have been the victors over us. I know of none more deserving and more meritorious than the soldiers who fight the battles of this country; and there is not a soldier of the Confederacy that I know of, but what is willing to see these men paid, and freely and cheerfully so. That is the sentiment of the country I represent. If the tide of battles had gone in the other direction, if our flag had floated forward instead of backward, we would have voted anything to those soldiers who won that fight; and if our soldiers are not pensioned, it is the fate of war. It is a risk which they took with the rest of us; and they bear their fortunes manfully in this, as they bared their hearts to danger during the war. There is no profession on earth that is not better paid than soldiery. I cannot afford, for one, to turn back because there may be frauds in the matter. If there be frauds it is a sad commentary on the law-making power that we cannot unkennel these frauds and strangle them."

Probably no words ever uttered by Mr. Garland in the Senate of the United States are more touching than his tribute to the dead senator from Wisconsin, Matthew H. Carpenter, the brilliant lawyer who had voluntarily and without remuneration helped Mr. Garland with his big case before the Supreme Court in 1866, and who had, on several occasions, befriended Arkansas. Mr. Garland had said of him at that time: "He was the very picture of striking manhood, his star was rapidly rising to its zenith, and great and brilliant intellectuality was stamped in unmistakable characters upon his face."

At his death Mr. Garland's eulogium was touching and beautiful, and full of allusions. We quote from the closing paragraphs:—

"In cursory reading a little while ago, Mr. President, I found a sentence, said to have been his production, which gives forth his view upon this thing we call life. It is this: 'The loves and friendships of individuals partaking of the frail character of human life may be shortly summed up: a little loving and a good deal of sorrowing; some bright hopes and many bitter disappointments; some gorgeous Thursdays and many dismal Fridays; some high ambitions and many Waterloo defeats, until the heart becomes like a charnal-house, filled with dead affections, embalmed in holy but sorrowful memories: and then the cord is loosened, the golden bowl is broken, the individual life is a cloud, a vapor that passeth away.'

"Probably this was the inspiration of one of those moments of sadness that at times come to us all. But it is a faithful summary at the last. His life, with its share of sorrows and trials and crosses, is full of good examples and noble encouragement to the young men of the land. Born and reared with no wealth, with no previous family name or prestige to rest upon, alone with his own great mind and energies, he rose from the very ground-work of society, and became one of the wonderful men of this wonderful age and country. On more than one ocassion did he serve in her troubles the State that honors me with a seat here; and the people of that State have a kind and tender rememberance of him, which will not be dimmed with the coming and going of the years. His loss to his country is great, and to his friends and family beyond estimate; but to all let the hope come that the tear-drop of sorrow that is shed today will be caught up and made to glow and sparkle in the rainbow of promise of tomorrow—without which hopes life's burdens and changes would be unbearable. His name and fame will be treasured tenderly in the land, and 'his memorial shall not depart away.'"

On the question of Chinese immigration Mr. Garland made a speech of considerable length on March 3, showing by argument and references to decisions of the United States Supreme Court and district courts, that the matter of legislating to exclude the Chinese, was a matter for Congress and not the States to perform. The acts of the States on the matter had been declared unconstitutional by the Supreme Court, he argued, and he quoted from Justice Field, showing that the matter was for Congress to act upon. He thought that the amendment under consideration, prohibiting the further naturalization of Chinese, ought to be adopted.

The bill to establish a Court of Appeals was discussed at great length in the sessions of May 2nd to 5th, and Mr. Garland spoke on each of these days. He stated that the purpose of these courts was, that they were to be localized and the proceedings brought home to the bosom and business of the people. The circuit judges who were to hold these courts already existed to some extent, and it was intended by the bill that the courts should be held to a particular locality, so that the judges might familiarize themselves with the jurisprudence, law and judicial policy of that particular section of the country. A proviso was introduced that no circuit or district judge before whom a case or question had been tried or heard in the district or circuit court below, should sit on the trial or hearing of such a case or question in the proposed appelate court. Mr. Garland favored this, and said that it was simply an oversight that it had not been put in the original bill. He said: "The idea is not founded as much on the pride of opinion of the judge as it is on a pure and simple question of justice to the litigant who appeals. When he appeals a case, as he would in this court, to six judges, he opens his case in the appelate court with one of the six judges against him, and to that extent he is denied a fair trial. Jurisprudence is the administration of justice according to the law. In the best days of Roman jurisprudence, they even tried all cases under a fictitious name. An upright judge has nothing in the world to do with knowing the parties in the court below. If one judge has already expressed his opinion, I do not care how able he may be, from Marshal down to the smallest man that ever disgraced a bench, it is human nature at least for him to contend for his own opinion."

On May 5, Mr. Garland spoke at great length, and his speech must have cost him many hours of work in preparation. He said that early in his senatorial career he had introduced a bill to change the Judiciary by establishing these intermediary courts, and that corporations in one State but doing business in another, if sued by the latter, should not have the privilege of removing the case to the United States Supreme Court. He said: "The importance and gravity of the question cannot be overestimated. We are now dealing with a very weighty subject, and the country is deeply interested in it. The repeal of all jurisdiction of the United States Courts over these municipal and quasi-municipal corporations is demanded by the necessities of the time, and is in strict account with the judicial system of the United States, organized by the Constitution and the Act of 1789 in pursuance hereof." Here followed a list of references to decisions of the Supreme Court in the matter. The earliest decisions showed that corporations are not "citizens" within the meaning of the Constitution, and hence cannot sue or be sued in a United States Court. Subsequent decisions, however, contradicted these. Mr. Garland said: "We have these contradictory decisions before us, to determine whether the one position is right, or the other. It is a decision which comes at last by construction. Anyway, if Congress gave to the Federal Courts jurisdiction over such cases as these, it can certainly take it away. Now, what is the reason why these corporations made under the State law, these quasi-municipal and municipal corporations, should have a place in the United States Courts? They are made under the State Laws; they are purely parts and parcels of the State's machinery, for the purpose of local government. Then why the necessity of going into the United States Courts, when you simply change your form? Upon any ground you may take it, as a pure question of right, these institutions should never have a place in the Courts of the United States. They should not be permitted to be sued there or remove their suits brought against them in the State Courts, when these suits are brought in the particular location where they are created by the States. I have thought on this question long and deliberately and patiently, and I think that these courts of appeal are necessary. With the vast increase of the business of the judiciary, with the vast addition of territory to the country, with all these questions as to public lands, questions of commerce brought about by the railroads, telegraphs, and such, I do not believe that the present judicial force will be sufficient, even if these courts are established." (Here followed an historical review citing opinions of men, bills to relieve the Supreme Court of circuit court duties, and acts extending the judiciary system, establishing new courts, etc., etc. Letters had been flooding Congress, asking for greater judicial force, etc.)

"Mr. President, think for a moment of the purpose of the act. It is not to establish principles of law, it is not to find the actual standard of right and wrong; but it is simply to say what the law is in a given case. It is not to write law-books for the profession; it is not to encourage litigation. Judges should not write law-books full of needless discussions. If I had my way, I would take the opinions back to the time of Coke, simply declaring that the facts in the case are such and such in the law; and I would not compel the judges to search from Colorado to Arkansas and then to New York, for some authority on the particular case. The purpose of a court is to establish what the law is in the particular case, and where the right is.

"I know that any bill of this sort will meet with objections; all bills do. This is something of a pioneer experiment; it is yet to be tested; it is to be tried in the crucible to see whether it will stand. After long and laborious examination of the question, I have laid before the Senate my honest convictions in reference to the whole question.

"Lawyers in my State and all others are clamoring for some relief. The Court of Appeals will take part of the rapidly increasing business of the country from the Supreme Court, and will act as a guard against bad judges in the lower courts. This will bring relief for some time to come—how long we cannot tell, because the country is growing, and it is an illustration at last of the fact that governments are not made, but grow as the country grows. I have stated honestly, fairly, and candidly to the Senate my views; with the additions and suggestions I have stated on it, I hope the bill now before the Senate will pass."

On May 22nd and 23rd, the Geneva Award Bill was up again, and Mr. Garland spoke again at some length, re-expressing his views, and enforcing the idea again that the matter should properly be referred to the Court of Claims, holding that that would be a legitimate solution of the matter and one with which all parties concerned would be satisfied.

On the bill to construct Mississippi River levees, which he himself introduced, Mr. Garland spoke at great length on March 15 and April 19. The bill provided for an appropriation by Congress of $15,000,-000. Mr. Garland argued that the matter was of national importance, and national in its nature. "The Mississippi is an inland sea," he said. "When the Southern States attempted to dissever themselves from the Union, no more powerful argument than the holding of the Mississippi prevailed against the success of those States.

"If a levee system is kept up in one way in Arkansas, in other ways in Mississippi, Tennessee, and Louisiana, it would be worse than no system at all. If these States had the authority to do this, they could not do it by conjunction or agreement, and hence are not able to meet this exigency.

"The Federal government would not yield the possession of this great river, in spite of all the forces the civilized world could muster and control; and if this river may be regarded in a certain sense as the property of the Federal government, why should it allow the states to build levees on it? The loss by the great flood of 1874, was the overflow of ten million acres of land, in the rich cotton, sugar and corn country. The recent overflow will cause a loss of at least one-third more, and will reach $30,000,000. When you come to measure the damages, there can be no estimate. If a failure of the cotton crop ensues from the overflow, not even our financial committee can estimate the loss to the whole country, not merely to Arkansas, Tennessee, Louisiana, Mississippi and Missouri, but to all commercial points and centers of business.

"It is necessary to proceed at once to give aid and start the building of levees, because, when the water recedes, thousands will have to wait three or four weeks before they can break up the ground to begin work; and if the government starts the work it can give employment to those thousands until that time. I say it with a serious conviction in my mind, that the splendid cotton country ranging from Crittenden County, Arkansas, to New Orleans, will have to be abandoned ultimately unless some assistance of this sort be given. The people will have to go to the poor hills. Fifty thousand people are houseless and shelterless, driven out and exiled. A great many of these, it is true, are colored people, who are fitted for that work by nature and by their calling in life, and in whose good strong arm there is more honest work than in any other known on the face of the earth. These are people needing to be provided for. Is is not time to do more than Congress has already generously done, in voting for temporary supplies for these suffering people, to institute the work and commence giving these poor men something to do immediately on the going down of the water?"

When Mr. Garland's bill had been returned by the Committee on Improvements of the Mississippi, that committee recommended $5,000,000, only one-third of what the bill asked for. Mr. Garland thereupon spoke

again, long and earnestly, showing that five millions
was not enough:—

"The President (Mr. Arthur) turned his face toward
the sun in his message, in not mentioning sections of
the Rebellion, just as the great Lincoln did, when he
requested his band, after he had taken the sword of
Lee, 'to play Dixie; it is ours also.' He was not
afraid of the slanders; he could hear that song played
which had stirred men to battle and caused valorous
hearts to kill his comrades. So President Arthur is
not afraid of any scarecrow of the Rebellion, and is
willing to restore the country ravaged by it.

"Is it economy to ask us to dribble on here from
time to time with a little appropriation, as though we
were clearing out a duck pond or a cat-fish pond in
Arkansas? Why help the men of these injured states?
Because they are citizens of this country. If they
honestly fought for what they thought to be right,
they had been overcome and have quit. Here is a
great man standing at the head of the Republican
party who says so; and whether either House of Congress allows it or not the country will applaud it
to the echo. 'Time at last makes all things even': no
question of that. I make the appeal upon the direct
right, law, justice, morals, common sense and conscience. The money is there in the treasury, received
from the tax on the cotton from this great valley; and
we ask you simply to give us part of it back. There
are sixty-eight million dollars in the treasury collected
from the Cotton Tax. Give us a mere pittance of one-
fourth. We are entitled to it. I have never belonged to
the school of strict constructionists. I have always
belonged to that school that fights for a sensible construction; and this is the sensible construction given
by Mr. Calhoun. If you can give land, can you not
give money? It was reached by Congress in the acts

of 1849 and 1850, and is reached by the Executive today.

"I want now to take all the chances there are under the report of the commission, like the man did, who, when he became seriously ill, sent for a preacher of every denomination, that he might have all the chances at going to heaven. I have on my table letters that would draw tears of blood from the hearts of men, if read, relative to the disastrous scenes which have accompanied the overflow that has come upon this country. We are poor. We may be poor through our own mismanagement and mistakes and faults, but we are poor. The States cannot build these levees now as they did in 1850. We need one uniform, compact system, and under the same authority, I beg Senators opposed to a large appropriation to come now and take a patriotic and magnanimous view of this whole subject. We are not working for today; nor for one section of the country; but for all time, and all the people of the earth. * * * The life of man is short, and events come thick and fast, and hurry on. In ten years from this day, if the appropriation of $15,000,000 is not made, I predict that Congress will vote fifty millions as cheerfully as they would vote five now. There is an urgent necessity for this work."

However, a little later, when it was apparent that Congress would not appropriate the full amount, Mr. Garland withdrew his amendment asking again for fifteen millions, saying that though he regretted to do it, he would nevertheless content himself for the present with five millions.

During the next session of Congress (1882-3) Mr. Garland managed to get three bills to pass both Houses. They were as follows:

A bill (S. Bill No. 2239) "granting right of way for railroad purposes and telegraph lines through the

lands of the United States included in the military reservation at Fort Smith, Ark." Introduced by Mr. Garland and referred to the Committee on Military Affairs,
reported back and passed the Senate, considered and
passed by the House, examined and signed, and
approved by the President.

A bill (S. Bill No. 2305) "authorizing the commissioner of the Freedman's Savings Bank and Trust
Company to examine certain claims against said company and to pay certain dividends barred by the act of
February 21, 1881, and for other purposes." Introduced
by Mr. Garland and referred to the Committee on
Finance, reported back, amended, and passed by the
Senate, passed by the House, examined and signed, and
approved by the President.

A bill (S. Bill No. 2412) "to encourage the holding
of a World's Industrial and Cotton Centennial Exposition in 1884." Introduced by Mr. Garland and
referred to the Committee on Agriculture, reported
back, amended, and passed by the Senate, passed by
the House, examined and signed, and approved by
the President.

In the early part of the session Mr. Garland spoke
at considerable length favoring the act providing for
a uniform bankruptcy law in the United States. We
shall not give all his arguments here, as they would
perhaps be tedious and uninteresting. They are marked
by a wealth of citations from history, cases in courts,
etc.; and show a great deal of study and detailed labor
on the subject. The debate lasted practically a month.
Mr. Garland said, in his concluding speech: "I believe
there is a general necessity in this country for a standing and fixed bankruptcy act. The jurisdiction was
given to Congress, and in view of what the different
States have done, Congress has seen proper from time
to time to pass bankruptcy acts, so that the creditor

from Georgia, the creditor from Arkansas, and the creditor from Ohio may all stand on an equal footing when they come into the court to have an estate of an insolvent distributed. That there is no great pressing demand for a bankruptcy act now, I do believe; but if you put it upon that ground simply, it is the very reason why the man in the song of the 'Arkansas Traveler' did not cover his house. He could not cover it when it was raining, and he didn't want to cover it when it was not raining, because then it didn't need it. If we wait until we get a stampede, cry, demand, and rush for such an act, the result will be that we shall get a patch work as we did in 1867; so that in six or seven years there will not be a show left of the original act, and we shall not even know out of what material it has been made. Now is the time to make the act, in time of peace, while there is no commotion and no distress in the country for such a special act."

In arguing for Civil Service Reform, on December 23, Mr. Grant went into considerable detail to show the restless state of the country. He said:

"If I had to interpret and summarize what was the cause of the verdict rendered by the people in the recent election, I would say that the country has become tired and restless and sore under the management of it in the harness and armor of war instead of that of peace. The country is like a man that is aged, lying upon one side for hours, who becomes restless and turn over on the other side so that he may enjoy his sleep and comfort further. It is like David equipped in the armor of Saul; it is encumbered and oppressed, and must necessarily sink under it. The legislation that was originated in time of arms to save the life of the country, as was said, is now the legislation for this time of peace; and that is the complaint of the country. This restlessness is not merely local, nor confined to one State. It is electricity all along the line; and—

> 'From peak to peak, the rattling crags among,
> Leaps the live Thunder! Not from one lone cloud,
> But every mountain now hath found a tongue,
> And Juno answers, through her misty shroud,
> Back to the Gorgeous Alps, who call to her aloud!'

"If there is no party adequate to the country's demand, it will create one. It may not be the Republican party nor the Democratic party. Octavious had a pary at one time in Rome, and Anthony had a party; but Rome had no party. It may be that here the interests of the country have no party. The verdict of the election may impart that, and if the Democratic party, now that it has these successes, addresses itself seriously and earnestly to this work, it will receive the applause and approbation of the country. If it does not it will not, and the country will seek a party which will accommodate itself to its demands."

A little later Mr. Garland said, referring more directly to the bill: "It is a mistaken idea that we can introduce a reform in this matter or any other, without hurting or affecting somebody. If we stood still and waited for the time to come to introduce reforms when nobody could be affected by them, we should never have one. The very demand and clamor for reform arises from the fact that some of the government officials need cleaning out. I for one believe that there are more employees in the government than there ought to be. I should like to cut down what I conceive to be the supernumerary of officials throughout the departments, who were put there by the necessities of war."

In the session of 1883-4, Mr. Garland was again appointed on the Judiciary Committee, the Committee on Territories, and the Committee on Epidemic Diseases; and was also placed on the Committee on Revolutionary Claims. During this session he was called several times to take the Vice-President's chair.

Out of the great raft of bills introduced by Mr. Garland at this session, only one got through both Houses of Congress, though many passed the Senate. It was a bill (S. Bill No. 1369) "to prevent and punish the counterfeiting within the United States of notes, bonds, or other securities of foreign governments." It was introduced by Mr. Garland and referred to the Committee on the Judiciary, reported back, passed the Senate, passed the House, examined and signed, and approved by the President.

Many of the petitions that he had presented in former sessions, and which had failed to be acted on and granted, he presented again in this, his last, session of the Senate.

Mr. Garland favored the bill providing that Congress give relief by appropriation toward eliminating the foot and mouth cattle disease in Kansas. He spoke on this bill March 14, 1884. He believed that Congress had the constitutional power to give this aid. He said, in part:

"You present me a calamity that is general in its character, and threatening to the country, that the local and domestic authorities cannot meet, and I vote to afford relief with as clear a conscience as I ever voted for any measure. If I did not believe we have the constitutional power there is no sympathy in my bosom—I believe I am as sympathetic as most men— that would induce me to violate the oath I took at yonder desk to support the Constitution. I act accord-ting to my interpretation of that instrument which I have sworn to support.

"Here is an industry now that is threatened with a prostration which will be worse than the failure of crops to the people who suffer from it; and it is not worth while to say, 'wait till the blow is struck and calamity done; then relieve it.' The sound of the fire bell is unpleasant, especially when you have to get up at night to go out and suppress the fire and endeavor to save life and property. We had better take precautions in advance, and not wait till these people come crippled here and say, 'Our industry is gone.'

"The power comes under the 'general welfare' clause of the Constitution. Where do you get the authority to build a Library Building? To erect the statues of great men, whose reputation in life has been won in killing their human brethren? Where did you get the power to give relief to the sufferers from the Mississippi flood? You got it under this clause, and nowhere else. Judge Story does not say that the 'general welfare' power in the Constitution rests upon any other power or is connected with it; it is an independent power. I read from the Constitution of the Confederate States where that was omitted for the express reason, as gentlemen of that school believed, that that power ought to rest upon other powers and be dependent on them; and they incorporated in that Constitution what is considered a fair and just interpretation of the Constitution of the United States upon this question.

"Judge Story, in adopting the language of Monroe and other presidents, adopts the language, first, beginning with Mr. Hamilton in his report on manufactures in 1791, and even that of Mr. Jefferson himself, who was the father of what we understand as the 'States' Rights' School, who worshiped States' Rights as devotedly as ever the Persian bowed before the eternal fires of the sky.

"This matter of eliminating this cattle disease is public or it is nothing. It is either a myth, a ghost, or it is general and public in its character. We have construed the Constitution, we have applied it time after time, year after year. It is now too late to say that we cannot apply it in this instance, when our country is threatened with a cattle disease. It is too late to question the authority. It is there, written in the text, for what is understood as the text is a part of it. It is written in the precedents which have become part of the law of the country.

"When we deal with this subject it branches into questions affecting commerce between the States. If we could, by some organic power, say that the cattle of Kansas alone would be affected by this measure, and none of any other State, we might get a resting place for the argument, but that cannot be done because it is a contagious disease.

"I have attempted to show that we have the authority to give help, under a fair, legitimate construction of the constitution; and by the precedents of former acts, it is put beyond any cavil or dispute."

Probably Mr. Garland's greatest speech in the Senate of the United States was his masterly argument of March 24, toward the close of the session, upon the bill (S. Bill No. 398) "to aid in the establishment and temporary support of common schools." The speech of Mr. Garland was on the amendment to the bill, (and involving substantially its merits) of Mr. Harrison of Indiana. In this great argument, we think, more than in any other debate in which he participated, he added the power of his great abilities as a constitutional lawyer to his ever-great earnestness and enthusiasm. The bill provided for the making of appropriations by Congress for the extermination of illiteracy in the states. It proposed to give $15,000,000 at once for the purpose, and diminish it by $1,000,000 every year for ten years, when it should cease. The money was to be distributed among the states in proportion to the number of persons within the school age in each, who were unable to read and write. It required that each State should spend of its own revenue one-third as much as it should receive from the United States; and then limited the amount to be expended to the support of normal schools to one-tenth of the amount received. It left the states free, under those restrictions, to expend the money according to their own judgment. Mr. Garland spoke at great length, favoring the bill, and we quote from him at length, owing to the general importance of the matter to the whole country, and the fact that much of his remarks are about the condition of his State. He said:

"In the discussion of the bill two questions naturally arise; first, the power to pass such a bill as this, and second, the policy of it. I do not require the thirteenth, fourteenth and fifteenth amendments to enable me to find the power of Congress to do this. I am satisfied that we had the power before the amendments were enacted. The point was decided by the Supreme Court, long before the amendments were ever dreamed of, in the case of Cooper vs. Roberts.

"Again, if Congress can grant lands for schools, it can certainly grant money itself. No fine-spun theory can bring an argument to show a distinction in the power to make the grant, as between money and land." (Here he cited cases of history before the amendments were enacted, to show that it had been the precedent and policy of the government to make appropriations

—that the power always existed and was never questioned.)

"If education is left with the states, it will never be carried on fully, or at least not for years to come. I believe every Southern state has come with proper guards to its Constitution and its statutory laws on the subject; but on account of the misfortunes to which they have been subjected, because of the poverty and great debts many of them bear, they cannot meet the exigency of the case. But that they have shown a willingness to do so as far as they can, in most cases, there can be no doubt. What is the problem before us? Illiteracy is the disease to be cured; this is the poison to be extracted, and it is right and proper to base the contribution upon that. You can fix no other standard so reasonable and fair. I feel assured in saying that without some safeguard on this subject not one of the Southern States could have been 'received back,' as Mr. Lincoln termed it, into practical relation with the other States of this Union. If one of these States had lingered or hesitated in the matter of education, it would not have been received back into the community of States. When the battle for the political life of the State of Arkansas was being fought, when the balance stood wavering here, persons unable to decide what should be its fate, gentlemen in the highest positions as officers of this land wrote to me to let them see our school law; and when I transmitted it there was no longer any doubt as to the fate of that struggle which was then going on for the political entity of the State of Arkansas.

"It was intimated that the proposed appropriation appeared to be in the name of the colored people, while in fact the whites would get the most of it. That is a mistake; there is no distinction there; the white and colored children share the contribution alike. They go into separate schools as a matter of course, which the courts in the different states have decided to be constitutional.

"The ratio of the payment of taxes in Arkansas is much greater than the white population to the colored. If I were now about to utter my last words, I should frankly say that there is no prejudice against the education of the colored children there, on the part of the educators, so far as I know. We may dispute as much as we please about the theoretical question, the oft-repeated one, whether the colored man can be educated; but in my judgment it is something that will never be settled. I know in many instances colored people have been educated, and I know that as citizens they have the franchise in their hands, and have a right to the honors of this government; and this being so, an effort should be made in the direction of elevating and improving them. If they are to be citizens, they should be made the very best citizens. They should know the value of the ballot that is put in their hands; they should know the value of civil rights. And for one, as I took the stump in favor of the present Constitution of Arkansas (the constitution of 1874), and was the first governor under it, I did not mean to humbug anybody then, nor do I mean to do so now. I want all races in the country to be brought up to the very highest phase of education, to the very front rank of knowledge. I do not believe, so help me Heaven, that there is any prejudice on the part of the educated classes in the State of Arkansas, to which my knowledge is principally confined, to the education of the colored people, as far and as much as the means given to them will enable them to do so. If we have done our best and are continuing to do so now, with this accumulated mass of population upon us, it seems to me there is but one duty, and that is to vote this aid.

"Mr. President, looking at the subject for myself, with all the lights that surround me, I do not know how my friends on the other side can say sincerely to the colored man, 'We want to educate you, and yet will not vote for this bill or something similar to it.' I do not know how they can make it clear to him that they are sincere when they withhold this effort to help him for ten years longer, until the States get upon a sound footing and wipe away the rubbish now resting upon them, and become self-sustaining.

"I look upon this measure as being the most important one that has been before Congress for many, many days; and for my State, I look upon it as being the most important bill to us that has been proposed here. We are struggling there with conscientious energy and with a high purpose to accomplish these ends. But by reason of circumstances not within our control, we are not able to meet the requirements of the time. Many of our schools hold sessions of only two or three months in the year. If this aid be given us, much good will be accomplished. We can meet in a reasonable and honorable way this great exigency. Are we together upon the great question of the day? Certainly, in the name of Heaven, after nearly twenty years of peace, we ought to be a unit upon some one question, and not be standing in the shadows of the past and fighting our battles over again, but be doing something for the advancing and fast approaching future. If we are really sincere, let us manifest our sincerity, and of all things it would be to me the best and proudest day since I have been here, to see this measure meet the entire approval of the Senate.

"In conclusion, I implore both sides and all sides to come together and vote for this bill and be a unit upon it, as we have been talking about it and promising it for years past."

And the bill finally passed the Senate in an amended form; but it got no further.

*   *   *   *

The above excerpts from the Speeches of Augustus H. Garland, though affording a poor ground upon which an estimate of his work in the Senate that would begin to do him justice can be based, will yet convey to the reader some idea of his thoroughness of attack, wealth of legal information, ability in presentation of facts, and earnestness of effort. Many short debates with Senators show his ability as a ready thinker, but of course have to be omitted. On many occasions he cleared up technical disputes and questions involving rules of order, or questions of legitimate procedure. His arguments served nearly always to straighten out the point under discussion, and to the evident satisfaction of those holding different views. He always had the rules of order at his finger's ends. With this he had a wealth of knowledge of precedents established by previous acts or procedures of Senate and House. He was ferquently referred to by his colleagues as "the able lawyer." Ex-Senator Berry of Arkansas says of him that he "was regarded by all Senators who served with him as one of the ablest lawyers who had served in the Senate since the war. He was universally liked, conservative in his views, and never got excited. He was likely to take just as fair a view of all possible questions as anyone."

Nothing is better evidence of the standing of Mr. Garland at Washington, than the personal testimony of men associated with him there, as that just quoted. Another gentleman who knew him there, the late Ex-Senator Jas. K. Jones, says of him: "He never sought to attract public attention to himself, and seemed to shrink from the public gaze. His speeches in the Senate show that his object was always to convince those to whom he spoke; and he never spoke over the heads of Senators to the people at large. He was a lawyer and a student, and had as little in him of what the word 'politician' is usually understood to mean, as any man I ever saw." He is said by some to have stood higher in the estimation of the Republicans, then in control of the Senate, than any other man from the South. He was regarded as being more of a patriot than a partisan; and his speeches, delivered with the rugged force characteristic of his temperament, carried great weight in consequence. By common consent, he was held to be one of the ablest exponents of the Constitution that ever sat in the Senate. He was on several occasions called to the Vice-President's chair to preside over the proceedings of that body.

SECTION III

In 1884 there came a call to Senator Garland to lay down his position of representing merely his State, and assume representation for the nation. President Cleveland appointed him Attorney General of the United States. This was a marked honor for Mr. Garland, and for his State as well; for this is the first and only time that Arkansas has been represented in the President's Cabinet. Not only that, but Mr. Garland enjoyed the distinction of being the first man from the South to sit in that body, after the War. When news of his appointment was received by his brother Senators, it seemed to give general satisfaction on all sides, and all thought that the President had made a wise choice. At this time Mr. Garland was considered one of the five most prominent Democratic leaders in the Senate. When he resigned and accepted the President's invitation to sit in his special council of advisors, it was felt all over the country that a man of rare ability had been added. He was a most prominent figure at Washington. His marked eccentricities of manner and method (of which we shall speak later), together with his great legal ability and capacity for making and holding friends, combined to attract to him an attention that was always a tribute to his high qualities.

Mr. Garland took up his official duties on March 6, 1885, and continued in office until 1889, when Harrison was elected to the Presidency. The pages following which contain some of his official opinions as Attorney-General, may not give that same interest that clusters around his magnificent speeches in the Senate. We have tried to pick out from the great raft of opinions given to the President by him, only those on the most important questions.

PARDON—LAWTON'S CASE.

Lawton, having been commissioned a lieutenant in the United States Army and taken an oath as such officer to support the Constitution, afterwards bore arms against the United States in the War of the Rebellion, but on February 6, 1867, received a full pardon from the President. Mr. Garland said, in reply to the President's letter: "The question for my opinion is, whether it was the intention of the fourteenth amendment to take away rights which previous pardons had restored; or in other words, whether its purpose was to cast a reproach on the Executive Department of the government by repudiating, as unworthy of credit, its acts of questionable validity, by destroying rights which had undoubtedly been vested under these acts, and by violating the national faith, so pledged.

"Applying the sound rule of interpretation given in the Supreme Court in various cases, to the third section of the fourteenth amendment, I am of the opinion that the consequences of allowing its general words of exclusion to operate without limitation in favor of persons in the situation of Lawton, would be injustice and a disregard of the public faith, which nothing short of the most explicit and controlling language should authorize.

"I am of the opinion that Lawton is not affected by the amendment, because at the time it was ordained the offences upon which the disability imposed is based, could not have been imputed to him, for the reason that he had by virtue of his pardon become a 'new man' and 'as innocent as if he had never committed the offence.' The effect of the pardon was to close the eyes of the law to it."

It will be recalled that the above case is somewhat similar to Mr. Garland's own position in 1867, when he argued the famous case of Ex Parte Garland in the Supreme Court of the United States.

Mr. Garland's opinion was asked for on the question whether an Indian, in the Territory, possessing otherwise the requisite attainments, but a member of one of the tribes there and not a citizen of the United States, could lawfully be appointed and qualify as postmaster of any of the several classes. He said: "Excepting as regards the offices of President and Vice-President and membership in Congress, the Constitution is silent on the subject of eligibility to office under the general government. Disqualifications are declared under particular circumstances, but there is no requirement in order to be eligible to office, other than an oath to support the Constitution. Hence, whether an Indian is eligible to the said office, depends on whether his status, civil and political, is at the time such that he can give the required bond and take the prescribed oath. Nothing in this oath precludes a foreign-born resident of the United States, who has not yet been naturalized, from taking it. Want of citizenship is not of itself an obstacle.

"But the condition of the Indian is peculiar. He is treated by our government as belonging to a separate, though independent, political community, and is not ordinarily dealt with by the general government as an individual, but as a member of a tribe. Unless clearly warranted by the provision of some treaty or statute, an act which thus interferes with the tribal relation, must be deemed to have no sanction in our laws.

"I therefore think that an Indian, while a member

of a tribe and subject to tribal jurisdiction, is not in legal contemplation competent to take the oath referred to."

The question was asked, whether the head-money tax of fifty cents, levied by the act of August 5, 1882, entitled "an act to regulate immigration," was demandable for passengers coming into our ports not as immigrants, but transiently, or tourists.

Mr. Garland said: "The question is, did Congress intend that the term 'passengers' should be taken in its most extended occupation, or in the restricted sense of immigrants coming for permanent abode?

"That Congress has power to lay an import of this kind has been recently decided by the United States Supreme Court in the 'Head-money Cases.' But this case involved only the constitutionality, and not the interpretation, of the act.

"Whenever Congress refers to persons entitled to its benefits, whether partakers of its bounty or objects of its protection, it invariably describes them as 'immigrants' and not as 'passengers.' On the other hand, when the statute would provide a protection against the introduction of convicts, lunatics, idiots and paupers, it declares that there shall be an examination into the condition of the 'passengers' using a term intended to include all other itinerants, as well as immigrants. I see nothing in the statute that leads me to believe that the word 'passengers' was intended to be taken in the restricted sense of immigrants, and it comprehends all itinerant persons."

GRANT TO GARLAND COUNTY, ARK.

Mr. Garland's opinion will fully explain the nature of the case:

"Under the circumstances existing in this case, and for reasons stated, the institution of proceedings on

Old Law Office of Judge Hubbard (still standing), Washington, Ark.

behalf of a certain land (part of the Hot Springs Reservation), granted to Garland county, Arkansas, for the site of a public building, would not be warranted.

"It is requested that 'legal proceedings be instituted, with a view to recover to the government the title and possession of the land, should the failure of the county authorities to carry out the purposes be regarded as operating to nullify the grant."

"While it is clear from the language of the grant that Congress intended to devote the land to the specific purpose; viz., ' to be used as a site for the public building of said county'; yet, whether this annexes a condition to the grant, or creates a mere trust, is not so clear. If a condition, upon breach thereof the grant would be liable to forfeiture; if a trust, the same result would not follow upon a breach.

"In the former case, I submit that in the absence of any law of Congress declaring the forfeiture or directing the institution of proceedings to that end, no authority exists to bring a suit in behalf of the United States to recover the land on the ground of failure to perform the condition. In either case, it would seem unnecessary to consider the subject of proceedings to enforce the trusts, as it appears that a suit has recently been brought to amend the aforesaid lease and recover control of the property, that it may be devoted to the purpose for which it was donated. These considerations lead me to think that, under the existing circumstances, I would not be warranted in instituting proceedings of any kind in behalf of the United States, touching the premises."

HOT SPRINGS RESERVATION—ARKANSAS.

"The Secretary of the Interior has power under the act of December 16, 1878, to lease sites upon the Hot Springs Reservation for the term of five years, and to relet the premises for the same term, from time to time, as the leases expire."

Upon the facts stated Mr. Garland advised: "That the Secretary may accept the surrender of a lease of a bath-house site heretofore made to Smithmeyer, and cancel the same, and then enter into a new lease of the premises to the same party for the term of five years.

"During the term of the lease, and while the tenant is in possession under the same, he may remove from the premises whatever improvements he has erected thereon for the purposes of trade, whether machinery or buildings; but if he leases the premises without removing such improvements, and the government should take possession, they would become the property of the latter."

MAIL CONTRACTS—DOUBLE PAYMENTS.

Hanger, of Little Rock, and others, were mail contractors for certain routes in the State of Arkansas, service upon which was discontinued May 31, 1861, up to which time, from January 1, 1861, they were paid by the government in full what was due them. Afterwards they collected from the State of Arkansas for the same service (January 1, to May 31, 1861), certain amounts, which were paid out of moneys belonging to the United States, which had been seized by the State.

Mr. Garland advised: "That the contractors are under legal liability to make restitution to the United States of the amounts so collected, but that their sureties cannot be held responsible therefore, upon the undertaking of the United States."

CLAIM OF A PARTICIPANT IN THE REBELLION.

In 1860, Eggleston, a naval officer, became entitled to a share in the proceeds of a captured slaver, the amount of which was certified to the Treasury Department by the Secretary of the Navy, but remained at the time unpaid.

In this case Mr. Garland advised: "That by force of the joint resolution of March 2, 1867, 'forbidding accounting officers settling claims existing prior to April 13, 1861, in favor of participants in the late insurrection or rebellion against the United States; payments of such shares cannot now be made, notwithstanding the President's proclamation of amnesty of December 25, 1868, and to authorize its payment, an act of Congrss, if necessary."

ATTORNEY GENERAL.

It was Mr. Garland's decision: "That the Attorney General of the United States (himself) will not interpret a regulation of practice made by the Commissioner of Patents for his own guidance and that of his subordinates for the conveniently intelligent and orderly disposal of the business of his office. Such regulations, which the heads of bureaus and departments can make, modify or amend at will, or enforce or waive, as seems expedient, may well be left for their interpretation to the head of the department or bureau to which they pertain."

Charles E. Holmes had entered the military service in August, 1862, as a volunteer, to serve for three years; he subsequently deserted; but he afterwards voluntarily returned to service under the President's proclamation (of pardon) of November 11, 1865, and was mustered out of service along with his company on July 2, 1865.

Mr. Garland advised: "That the time which had elapsed between his desertion and his return (with payment therefor) should not be credited to him in a discharge or otherwise, but he is entitled to have his actual service credited to him in an honorable discharge."

An opinion of some importance and interest which Mr. Garland gave, was with reference to the protection of the law afforded to foreign consuls, resident in the United States.

He advised: "That a foreign consul, a resident of the United States, must look for protection to his person and property to the laws of the State in which he resides. The laws which protect the President of the United States in his person and property, are the same as those which protect the humblest citizen; and if the personal or property rights of that high functionary should ever be violated in the City of Cincinnati, he would have to look for protection to the laws of the State of Ohio. Certainly a foreign consul cannot justly complain because he is not better protected than the highest officer of the government of the United States."

On the general subject of the ownership of real estate in the Territories by aliens, on a case which came up, Mr. Garland gave the following opinion, which will explain the case in question:—

"The provision of the act of March 3, 1887, Chap. 340, restricting the ownership of real estate in the Territories to American citizens, etc., applies to mines, these being real estate.

"But stock in a corporation is personalty, and consistently with these provisions an alien may hold shares of stock issued by an American corporation owning mineral lands in the Territories; yet where the holding by aliens exceeds twenty per cent of its stock, such corporations can neither own, nor hold hereafter, acquired real estate, while such holding by aliens in excess of twenty per cent continues.

"So an alien may hereafter advance money for the purpose of developing mining property in the Territories; but he cannot thereby acquire any interest in such real estate. An alien may lawfully contract with an American owner to work mines by a personal contract for hire, on a bona-fide lease, for a reasonable time."

In a case concerning the Kansas and Arkansas Valley Railroad Company, Mr. Garland advised:—

"That under the act of June 1, 1866, Chap. 395, authorizing said railroad company to construct a railroad through the Indian Territory, the company has no right to go beyond the limits of the right-of-way therein prescribed, for the purpose of taking timber or other material for the construction of such railroads.

"The courts named in the eighth section of that act have jurisdiction over the controversies between said company and the Cherokee Nation growing out of the taxing timber or other materials by the former, beyond said limits. But the right of the Cherokees to go into Court does not diminish in any degree the duty of the Executive Department of the government to use its power for their protection by ordering the encroachments of the railroad company to be stopped."

Mr .Garland gave three important opinions relative to the general subject of "Retired List of the Army." The facts of each case are herewith given, together with the opinions, in their order.

(1)

Isaac Lynde, a major in the Seventh Infantry, was, by direction of the President, dropped from the rolls of the Army November 25, 1861; and H. W. Waller, a captain in the Fourth Infantry was, with the advice and consent of the Senate, appointed major in the Seventh Infantry, in Lynde's place. Afterwards, on November 27, 1866, the President revoked the order dropping Lynde, and directed that he be restored to his former commission, to fill a vacancy of major in the Eighteenth Infantry, to date from July 28, 1866; and at the same time, by direction of the President, Lynde was placed on the retired list as major.

Mr. Garland advised: "That the action of the President on November 27, 1866, was ineffectual to restore Lynde to the Army and place him on the retired list, and he is not entitled to be borne thereon."

(2)

Charles B. Stivers, a captain in the Seventh Infantry, was summarily dismissed from the service by direction of the President, July 15, 1863, and notified thereof. Afterwards, on August 11, 1863, the order of dismissal was revoked; whereupon Stivers, the vacancy not having been filled in the meantime, returned to the position from which he had been dismissed and continued to serve therein until December 30, 1864, when, upon the finding of a retiring board, he was retired under the provision of the Act of August 3, 1861.

Mr. Garland advised: "That the dismissal of July 25, 1863, created a vacancy which could not otherwise be filled than by appointment, with the advice and consent of the Senate; that the subsequent revocation of that order on August 11, 1863, was ineffectual to restore Stivers to his former position in the Army; that afterwards, when he was put on the retired list, he was not a commissioned officer of the Army; and that, accordingly, he is not entitled to be borne on such list."

(3)

James .T. Leavy, a first lieutenant in the Seventh Infantry, having been found by a retiring board "incapacitated from active service on account of insanity, which insanity is not incident to the service," was by direction of the President, retired July 31, 1868, on pay proper alone under the act of August 3, 1861. At Leavy's request the order of retirement was by direction of the President, on June 23, 1869, so amended as to wholly retire him from service with one year's pay and allowances. On April 2, 1878, by direction of the President, the order of June 23, 1869, was declared void, on the ground that Leavy was insane when he requested it; and he was restored to the retired lists in accordance with the original order.

Mr. Garland advised: "That after the President had once acted upon the finding of the retiring board, by placing Leavy on the retired list with pay proper alone under the act of August 3, 1861, his power over the case was exhausted, and the subsequent order wholly retiring Leavy was void for want of authority thus to retire him, and that therefore Leavy is entitled to be borne on the retired list conformably to the order retiring him to pay proper alone under the Act of August 3, 1861."

An interesting case upon which Mr. Garland gave advice, and with which we shall conclude our brief treatment of his opinions as Attorney General, comes under the head of "Double Pensions." A person to whom pension was granted as the widow of a soldier in the War of the Rebellion, was also granted a pension certificate as the widow of a soldier in the War of 1812; and drew pensions upon both certificates from March 9, 1878 to December 3, 1883. The Commissioner of Pensions, on discovering this, required her to make an election; and she, having elected to hold the first mentioned certificate, he ordered the amount which had been paid to her on the other certificate to be withheld in installments of six dollars per month from payments thereafter, and issued an order to the Pensions Agent accordingly.

Mr. Garland advised: "That the order made in this case, being within the general jurisdiction of the Commissioner, is obligatory on the Pensions Agent, and that the accounting officers of the Treasury have no power to disallow payments made by the agent pursuant thereto.

"It is not within the province of the accounting officers of the Treasury, upon hearing of any order made by the Commissioner of Pensions to a pension agent for the payment of pensions, to notify such agent of what their decision will be upon his account when rendered.

"In the case stated, the whole of the monthly pension under the certificate which the pensioner elected to hold should be withheld until the amounts so withheld shall equal the sum paid the pensioner under the other certificate."

*   *   *   *

Mr. Garland's career as Attorney General was slightly crippled by the vials of slander heaped upon him by inimical newspapers, etc., because he owned three hundred dollars of Pan-Electric telephone stock. He had just entered his acceptation of President Cleveland's offer to go into the Cabinet, when these newspapers began to circulate a slander as unfounded as untruths can ever be. He had bought a few shares of this company's stock while a Senator, and others who had done the same were Isham G. Harris of Tennessee and Joseph E. Johnston of Georgia. Now the Bell Telephone Company was a wealthy concern, and with its countless thousands determined to try and choke out the smaller Pan-Electric Company; and it was therefore to its interest to fight all the men connected with it, by the false slander of good men. Because of Mr. Garland's special prominence, most of the accusations fell on him. But when he found that he was the subject of all these charges, he went frankly to President Cleveland, as only a manly man could do, and laid the whole matter before him, offering to resign on the instant if the President should think it best. Cleveland took it under advisement, and then told Mr. Garland that his holding of the stock was in no way incompatible with his holding the office of Attorney General.

The House of Representatives took the matter under investigation, urged on by the Bell Telephone interests there; but it resulted in the entire vindication of Mr. Garland and the others. This statement is based on a careful study of the proceedings of the Committee appointed by the House of Representatives "to investigate charges against certain public officers relating to the Pan-Electric Telephone Company and to suit by the United States to annul the Bell Telephone patents." The committee was composed of Mr. Boyle, of Pennsylvania, Mr. Cates of Alabama, Mr. Eden, of Illinois, Mr. Hall, of Iowa, Mr. Hale, of Missouri, Mr. Ramey, of Massachusetts, Mr. Millard, of New York, Mr. Hornback, of Kansas, and Mr. Moffatt, of Michigan.

Later years have only strengthened the decision of the committee. Mr. Garland could not have been justly criticised; but slander can be circulated on the bravest, and it sometimes takes a long statement to clear those bravest to the public satisfaction. It gives newspapers, if inimical, the opportunity to say something to their liking. But while Mr. Garland's reputation suffered some among strangers, and very slightly among some former friends—the thing which hurt him most—yet he retained the fullest confidence of those who knew him well. Honest, fearless, resolute, he did not shirk a duty or responsibility to avoid criticism.

From 1889, when Mr. Garland retired from the office of Attorney General of the United States, until his death in 1899, he practiced law at Washington. Nearly all of his practice was before the Supreme Court. In these later years public office had no charm for him and he preferred to settle down to the quiet practice of the law. It is authentically stated that he was several times, the principal one perhaps being at the death of Justice Wood, in May, 1887, offered a place on the Supreme Court bench, but refused on account of his advanced age and declining health. He was also asked to take a place on the Interstate Commerce Commission, but again refused. His services were much in demand at Washington by those who sought a correct interpretation of the organic law of the land. He was a power before the United States Supreme Court. He was said to be one attorney who always made clear to the Court the law in the case he argued. In some of the cases which he presented to that body he obtained decisions in accordance with his views, the result having had their effect upon all citizens of the Republic; and never to their detriment. His influence at Washington was far-reaching. He wrote a little book in 1898, one year before his death, entitled, "Experiences in the Supreme Court," in which he tells of the cases in which he had participated before that tribunal. Probably his two most notable achievements in the law, were the cases of Ex Parte Garland, of which we have already given a full account, and the case of Osborne vs. Nicholson, in which the validity of contracts for slaves was established.

Mr. Garland was in very poor health for several years preceeding his death, and some months before the end had been confined in the Hospital for several weeks. His friends noticed when he was able to be out again that he had failed rapidly and was growing feeble. A few weeks before he died he was taken ill with the grip, and had suffered from its effects very much. He doctored himself by taking popular remedies, and did not consider his case serious enough to call in a physician. The day before his death, while in the Supreme Court room, he had laid his hand on his head and complained of being very ill.

On the morning of January 26, 1899, before going into the Supreme Court room, he spent some time in the Clerk's office, and remarked to one of the officials that he was not feeling very well, and thought he would go to Fortress Monroe on the following Monday to take a rest. But he did not regard his condition at the time as being at all serious.

The strange manner of Mr. Garland's death while pleading a case before the Supreme Court of the United States, is known to all. There is no late parallel to the manner in which he received the final summons, except the case of Wm. H. Windom, former Senator from Mississippi and Secretary of the Treasury, who succumbed to apoplexy some years before, at the conclusion of a speech delivered at the annual banquet of the New York Chamber of Commerce. Mr. Garland was stricken with apoplexy while addressing the court, at fifteen minutes past twelve in the afternoon, and died within ten minutes. The occurrence came with startling unexpectedness, changing the usual calm and dignity of the Court into temporary confusion, while the dying man was carried from the chamber in a futile effort to alleviate his condition. When the Court convened at noon Mr. Garland resumed an argument in the case of Lawson vs. Moore, which had begun the day before. There was a full bench, with the exception of Justices Brewer and White. Mr. Garland spoke calmly, and with no evidence of agitation or effort. He had read from a law volume and had followed with the sentence. "This, your honors, is our contention." As the last word was uttered he was seen to raise his hand and then gasp. He tottered and fell sideways, striking against a chair and overturning it as he fell heavily to the floor. His associate in the case, Mr. Frank Mackey, was at once by his side. A deadly pallor had overspread his face, giving place to a purple which foretold the gravity of the attack. He was carried from the chamber across to the room of Chief Clerk McKinney, and all that was possible was done to save his life. Within ten minutes from the time of the stroke Mr. Garland breathed his last.

Word of the tragedy was soon noised through the Capitol, and Senators and Representatives hurried to the Court room. The two Senators from Arkansas, Mr. Berry and Mr. Jones, were among the first to view the body, and following them was a long line of persons high in legislative and legal circles, who had been associated with Mr. Garland at various times in his long and notable career of public services.

Thus did "that mysterious monarch, that with the self-same tread knocks at the doors of King's palaces and poor men's huts," invade the sanctuary of justice for Augustus H. Garland. No spot in all our land is so replete with solemn memories as that on which he fell. Here were solved by the calm light of reason and unbiased equipoise of the law, many of the most momentous questions that have ever been submitted to mortal tribunal. This was for a long time the Senate Chamber of the United States, and here were delivered the great speeches of Clay, Webster and Calhoun. This was undoubtedly the fittest place for the ending of so great a life.

Mr. Garland closed his earthly career in the presence of what he had often called the highest and purest tribunal upon earth. The late Ex-Senator James K. Jones said of the manner of his death: "I am sure that if Mr. Garland had been consulted, the manner of his death was exactly what he would have preferred." Just after Mr. Garland's death, former Judge Henry W. Scott of New York recalled a conversation held with him in Washington some two months before. "You have expounded many great constitutional questions in this tribunal," remarked Judge Scott, "You may yet die in the harness." In reply Mr. Garland said, "It has been over forty years since I argued my first case. Nothing would please me better, when my time comes to die, than to be stricken right here in this court room in the midst of an argument. That would be a fitting climax to my career." It was almost on the same spot where this conversation occurred, that Mr. Garland fell dead while arguing his case. The Arkansas jurist died a husbandman, falling between the handles of his plow, a pilot dropping lifeless at his wheel, a philosopher breathing his last among his books. He died at his work, in the highest forum of the American lawyer's fame.

Mr. Garland's body was embalmed the evening of January 26, remaining at the undertaker's that night. The next morning it was removed to the Colonial Hotel and rested until Saturday morning, when the funeral train started for Little Rock, which place it reached on Monday following. The body was interred at Mount Holly Cemetery, where his wife, who died in

1877, and his daughter, Miss Daisy, who died at Washington, D. C., were buried.

In former years Mr. Garland had mixed freely with the people, and everybody knew and loved him. All of his early associations were with Arkansans; and though he was occupied at the nation's capitol almost constantly since his entrance to the Senate in 1877, yet he still retained up to the end his citizenship in his State, and loved to return and be welcomed by his people at home. During his long service in public life, he had a hold on the affections of his people which could not be shaken. At the time of his death no citizen of Arkansas was held in higher esteem than he. Loved and respected by the people of the State, and honored by the nation, in every position he occupied he acquitted himself of his duties like a patriot. It was therefore no wonder that his memory received such homage when his people were given a last opportunity to demonstrate their respect for the great statesman by performing in appropriate manner the offices due the dead. Mr. Garland was popular with all classes. The humblest citizen was his friend and admirer, and none exhibited grief more sincere at his bier than the artisan and the wage-earner. Among the visitors at his funeral were prominent men from all parts of the State, who had journeyed there on the special mission of paying tribute to the distinguished dead. The dreary weather in no wise held back the people. The large attendance was emblematic of the high esteem in which all Arkansas held Mr. Garland, and of the popular appreciation of his eminent services to the State. Many colored people called to take a last look at the face. Not a few of them were typical old Southern negroes, who gratefully remembered occasions when Mr. Garland had spoken kindly to them.

The above attempt at faithful account of the public record of Mr. Garland has been made with the consciousness that it would be superfluous to try to compress into a brief compass anything but the principle event of the life that forms a part of the history of the State of Arkansas, and the country at large— a life comprising a remarkable series of triumphs over difficulties and obstacles that often seemed insuperable. Mr. Garland lived very much in the public eye. A considerable part of his life was spent in a very strong period of our history, during which time he was constantly taking a prominent part in State and national affairs. In his position he was necessarily exposed to criticism on the part of political enemies and inimical newspapers; but under the most trying conditions the fairness and uprightness of his intentions shielded him from reproach. He could never be accused of having any personal aim in view, but was always devoted to the duties of the hour, with the confiding belief that deeds well done will generally bear their own good fruits. He performed the various tasks confronting him with entire singleness of purpose. He was always jealous of the honor of his State; and, in 1880, he spoke in nearly every county, opposing with all his might the Fishback Amendment, which repudiated the "Holford Bonds," which were for years a source of trouble to the State. He believed that it was neither honest nor honorable for the State to refuse to pay these bonds. (See Shinn's History.)

We have reserved for this place to say something of Mr. Garland's personal appearance and characteristics. In person, he was well-built and tall. His head was large and his face round and smooth-shaved, and animated with black and most expressive eyes. His smooth and excellent features indicated an amiable disposition. Strength and dignity were portrayed in his very countenance. Like most great men, his tastes were simple and his manners plain. He was at home anywhere, whether in the dignified precincts of the Federal Supreme Court, in the Senate, in the presence of the autocratic President of the United States, or in the modest unpretentious surroundings of "Hominy Hill," his twelve thousand-acre plantation home, situated twelve miles from Little Rock. In his personal traits, Mr. Garland was one of the most amiable Democratic men that ever entered public life. While serving as Attorney General, he lived in an old frame house with large grounds, on Rhode Island Avenue, near Fourteenth Street. Visitors to his residence on summer evenings would find him usually with his coat off, enjoying relaxation, walking about his lawn or sitting in the shade, looking like a prosperous farmer after a hard day's work. He often told his friends that "Hominy Hill" in Arkansas was a more delightful place than the most elegant house at the national capital. Mr. Garland's gaunt figure, strong face, old-fashioned rolling collar, long broad-cloth coat and wide sombrero, made him a conspicuous figure at Washington. He was a familiar personage at the capital for more than twenty years. Mr. Garland was a charming character, and his many friends were devoted to him not because he was a great man, but because he was true and possessed those traits of character indispensable to noble manhood. His wife had died in 1877, but his mother lived with him at Washington. She is said never to have seemed fatigued in the entertainments of her son's visitors and friends. She always received them with the same cordiality as though they were calling on them in their simple home in Arkansas. They constituted a most openhearted and affectionate family. Warm and earnest in their friendship, genial in companionship, no one ever

visited them who failed to take away and carry always
kind remembrances of them. Mr. Garland's tastes
were simple and inexpensive, and he cared nothing
for wealth. His principal care was to keep always and
scrupulously out of debt.

Mr. Garland was a man of many eccentricities. In
a way he was as eccentric as Samuel Houston or
Andrew Jackson. He habitually refused to wear a
dress coat, and more especially so after the death of
his wife. When he accepted President Cleveland's
offer to go into the Cabinet, he made it a condition
that he should not be required to participate in any
of the social functions. And this pledge was kept,
for during the four years in which he was Attorney
General, he never appeared at any of the official entertainments. During his entire life at Washington, he
never accepted nor offered formal hospitality. But he
often dropped in to dinner with a neighbor, or asked
a friend to go home and take "pot luck" with him. A
written invitation was always declined, no matter what
it was nor from whom it came. He abhorred conven-
tionalities; but this did not prevent him from being
acknowledged by his peers in the legal profession as
being one of the most capable men who ever filled the
place of Attorney General. He used to say that his
idea of hospitality was a cob pipe and a jug of whiskey. He took the ground that no true Democrat ever
took liquor out of a bowl or glass. But curiously
enough, he was a total abstainer from all spirit and
malt liquor. When someone asked him how he could
cultivate a habit so much at variance with his principles, he said: "I used to drink as regularly and fre-
quently as any one. But one day while walking
through the cemetery at Little Rock, I saw the new-
made grave of a bright man, who had been a friend
from boyhood. I suddenly realized what brought him

there, and I remembered that several others of our age had gone before, from the same cause. It occurred to me that I had drunk quite as much liquor as they, and that I had had my share."

Another of his peculiarities was his intense hatred of doctors. He used to say that until he broke his leg (about a year before he died) he had never paid a doctor's bill nor paid a cent for medicine. He believed that the medical profession was a sort of humbug; that no man was ill unless he abused himself; and that he could be cured by correcting that abuse. While he was Attorney General he was inflicted by a swelling of the jaws. He got a notion that he had been poisoned in some way, and his associates persuaded him to go to a doctor. The physician looked him over and remarked: "There is nothing serious the matter with you. You have only a mild case of mumps." "Hell, mumps!" exclaimed Mr. Garland in a rage. He stamped out of the office in high indignation, but by the advice of friends remained in the house two or three days, to avoid catching cold until the swelling had gone down.

Mr. Garland was a practical joker, a thorough judge of human nature, and a very keen observer of the ridiculous and artificial in men. Association with him was a constant round of pleasant and instructive past-time. To great qualities of mind he added an unstudied dignity, the gentleness of a woman, and the charm of spontaneous humor. He was playful as a boy, and fond of candy as a school-girl. He was very hard to practice a joke upon. On one ocasion some of his friends in the Senate, knowing Mr. Garland's love of chocolate candy, a sack of which he nearly always had upon his desk, procured some blocks of soap resembling candy, and placing them upon his desk, waited until he should come in and eat them. Mr.

Garland saw the luscious blocks laying before him when he entered the chamber, and immediately began eating one. But Senators who were waiting for him to go to the door to cast out the offending "chocolate," were disappointed. Mr. Garland, noticing the joke, quietly sat in his place, chewed it, and as quietly swallowed, just as though nothing out of the ordinary had happened; thus turning the joke on his friends.

Mr. Garland was very fond of the quiet sport of angling. He also loved to hunt with his friends. Lawyers used to travel by the military road from Little Rock to Arkadelphia, and Mr. Garland with his friends would stop at the old "Brick House" on the Caddo river near Arkadelphia and pitch camp there; though generally he himself would come on to Arkadelphia, and stay with his relatives. He often came down from Little Rock to go hunting and fishing with some of his friends.

Mr. Garland was a man of very strong family relations, and the center of all his thoughts was the domestic hearthstone. His later years were much saddened by the suicide of his daughter, which has never been fully explained. The sorrow over the loss of his wife, who passed away at Christmas time in 1877, he carried with him through the rest of his life. Many sorrows and bereavements fell to his lot during the years just preceeding his death. He was just recovering from a painful accident caused from falling on the ice. For months he lay upon his back and "reckoned he never was going to get well." In his last years he paid many sad tributes to humanity, full of depth of thought, and a pathos that was profound. His closing of life was marked with domestic afflictions which his affectionate nature would not permit him to forget, and whose bitterness time could not alleviate. We recall from the Congressional Record several instances

when, in the Senate, he referred to his family joys and
sorrows, in a passing way. And yet he looked up
through sorrow to joy, and would not permit himself
to be overwhelmed by any disaster. On one occasion
he said in the Senate, "It will not do, in the hurried
march of events of human life, to linger too long at
the graves of departed friends. Probably we all do
too much of that." His was a faith that necessitated
a hereafter in which all the disappointments of this
world are healed, and all its sorrows palliated.

Augustus H. Garland was in many respects the
greatest man that Arkansas ever produced. In some
ways his life is a parallel to that of Washington.
Born in 1832, just one hundred years after the birth
of the "father of his country," he likewise died in 1899,
a century after the great Virginian's passing. Garland was to Arkansas something of what Washington
was to the nation. His aid in making real the recu-
peration of the State under his administration as the
first governor under the new constitution, and caus-
ing it to be finally and fairly started upon its upward
course of prosperity and peace, bears an unusual anal-
ogy to the great mission of Washington to the infant
Republic. Like Washington, in a lesser degree to be
sure, he represented both his State and Nation, and
in no position given him was he ever found wanting.
Knowing no creed, he yet loved his fellow man, and
demonstrated it at the very time when it tried mens'
souls to do so. Like Washington, he took all his public offices practically without opposition, and as responsible gifts. Whenever he manifeted a willingness to
serve, his nomination followed, almost by acclamation.
The great estimate of his abilities and personal merit
is sufficiently attested by the fact that he never at any
time encountered any serious opposition. Few men in
public life have been more highly honored, and few, if

any, maintained so strong a hold on a constituency. Occupying many and exalted positions in public life, and filling them all to the satisfaction of the public, he was modest and unassuming at all times, and under all circumstances a plain, matter-of-fact, practical man, and not the least puffed-up by the honors which had been showered upon him. The high places to which he was often called by the voice of his fellow-citizens furnishes good evidence that he secured and maintained through life that cordial appreciation aroused and sustained by the union of mental vigor and personal worth. And he performed the various tasks with unswerving singleness of purpose and conspicuous talents. Arkansas loved him, because he was one of the truest friends the commonwealth ever had. The quarter of a century in which he served his country as a statesman was a period in our country's history which is rich and important in great events; a period which in industrial development, in expanding commerce, in the advancement of education, in the betterment of civilization, was more eventful than any like period in our national history. As Governor, in the Senatorial halls, in the President's Cabinet, before the Supreme Court, everywhere he stood as the embodiment of

"That providence which in a watchful State,
  Knows almost every grain of garnered gold;
  Finds bottom in the uncomprehensive deep,
  Keeps pace with thought, and almost like the gods
  Does thoughts unveil in their dumb cradles.
  There is a mystery in the soul of State,
  Which hath an operation more divine
  Than breath or pen can give expression to."

There was but little in Mr. Garland's nature that was dogmatic. Though he held consistently to opinions which he had from mature deliberation, yet he was so tolerant of others' views that he was exceptionally free from that extreme partisan spirit which is often considered necessary for those who desire political success. He always enjoyed the support of his own party, and often got that of his adversaries. From first to last he was more of a lawyer than politician, using the word in its popular sense. He believed in the principles of his party, yet he was never a partisan in the sense that he was not in touch with the people's welfare, irrespective of party prejudice. He never wavered in his allegiance to his profession. Unlike most lawyers who turn from the forum of the court room to engage in political battles, he always maintained an unbroken intercourse with the courts at bar, and still found an unabated pleasure in the writings of a long line of illustrious jurists. These were the companions of his solitude. After the great authors of jurisprudence, he loved to read the fathers of the Constitution. That instrument was always the rock upon which his feet rested. Mr. Garland was not at any time a great general or miscellaneous reader of literary work, but he had a few favorite authors whom he would read and reread with ever-increasing admiration and affection. Nevertheless he gathered during his life-time a library of some three thousand well-chosen volumes, exclusive of his law library. In this he took great pride. After his death this library was put on the market and the books were widely scattered, some going to the libraries of Hendrix and Ouachita Colleges, but the larger part, and especially his rare books and those containing autographs of celebrities, went to New York.

Mr. Garland never was a conspirator; nor did he ever entertain a thought in public life that was not for the good of Arkansas. He never shirked a responsibility when the honor of his State was at stake. Senator Hoar, with whom he had engaged in many a debate over matters in the Senate of the United States, said upon motion of Senator Jones that that body take a recess in order that Senators might attend Mr. Garland's funeral: "Mr. President, it will perhaps not be inappropriate for some gentleman on this side of the chamber to express the great affections which his old associates here felt for this eminent gentleman who died so suddenly in the heigth of his intellectual vigor, in the capitol itself. He was a model of the Senatorial character; an admirable lawyer; a statesman whose vision and interest comprehend the whole country, without distinction of section or party; a man full of patriotism and unimpeachable personal integrity; a model not only of the character of the Senator, but of the character of the gentleman." The above is an admirable summary of what might be termed a practical view of Mr. Garland's life and character. That he had faults and made mistakes is simply to say that he shared in the common infirmities of humanity; but they were far outweighed by clear judgment, a mind of unusual strength, and many shining virtues which greatly endeared him to those he represented. He was a manly man, ever-approachable, though possessing great courage in his convictions; and while urging them with a zeal born of honest belief, he had the inestimable faculty of winning adherents by strength of presentation, blended with suavity of manner. He was conspicuous in the fact that his broad soul expanded with tender and affectionate regard for the poor and humble.

The world would be poor indeed without the memories of its mighty men. In honoring great men, a nation or state but honors itself; for great men are the index-fingers of the country's greatness. They form the channels through which we pass; they shape our destiny. Above, all citizens of a country like ours, or any country for that matter, should honor the brave and independent spirit, and the man of great integrity. The very character of a civilization comes to flower and fruit in the wealth in its literature of tributes to its mighty dead. Mr. Garland stood at the very summit of his power when stricken down—the peer of the greatest. An orator always logical and intense, sometimes even picturesque, he had always the "indefinable something" men call presence. He was an absolutely honest man, and one whose principles could not in any way be bought. He believed that betrayal of trust is the death of the nation. In Congress at a time most trying in our history, when men in high places were being contaminated, he went in and came out without charge or suspicion on his character. Above all, he kept ever and always the company of his self-respect. Faithful and incorruptible, he was an ideal statesman, and representative. He was proud of his State, and his State is justly proud of him. He gave to his country his highest service, his deepest thought. Let the country therefore honor him with monumental shafts—fit emblems of structures already built in human estimation by the intensity of conviction and unswerving courage of the man.

The public career of Augustus H. Garland is a rich volume of true greatness. His record is a part of the history of his country. We trust it will ever be an inspiration to youth and admiration to age. His career is closed. His passing repeats "the old story that is retold in every flower that blooms and every leaf that falls—that all our strivings, ambitions, contentions, victories, have for their exhibition only a narrow and temporary stage; and the actors themselves, and the objects for which they contend, are alike but for a day."